IRIS AND ME

IRIS AND ME

PHILIPPA WERRY

ahoy!

to my cousin Louise, traveller and friend

Cover art by Sarah Pou.
Cover design by Sarah Bolland.
Edited by Mary McCallum.
Typesetting and book design by Paul Stewart.

A catalogue record for this book is available from
the National Library of New Zealand. Kei te pātengi
raraunga o Te Puna Mātauranga o Aotearoa te
whakarārangi o tēnei pukapuka.
ISBN 978-1-99-115084-4

Printed in Aotearoa New Zealand by Ligare.

AHOY!
an imprint of The Cuba Press
Box 9321 Wellington 6141
Aotearoa New Zealand

This book deals with themes of depression and suicide.
If you or someone you know needs help,
call Lifeline (0800 543 354), Youthline (0800 376 633)
or 0800 What's Up? (0800 942 8787).

This is the story

of a long journey
and a true friend.

It is the story of other things, too:
sisters (three)
ships (many)
secrets (a multitude).

A child; another child.
Work. Words.
And a Hermes portable typewriter.
We are a team, the three of us:
my friend, the typewriter and me.

Words are amazing, don't you think?
I used to wonder at how we all have the same
language, the same alphabet,
the same letters, and turn out so many different words.
But then we set off on our long journey
and I realised, of course, that isn't true.

There are many languages, many alphabets,
many scripts, many letters,
and so many words.

I don't have a name of my own,
but my friend does.
Her name is Iris.

Iris, my friend.
A maker of words.

Iris knows the power of words,
and what they can do.
Words, she says, *should be hard old lamps,
and white of wick,
and the right flame rises then.*

Beginnings

Where was this long journey
and where did it take us?
On how many ships,
carrying how many secrets?

And who am I, anyway?
Isn't that what you are asking yourself?

Don't worry,
I will tell you everything
all the way to the end,
or as far as we have got, anyway.

But where is the beginning?
Should I start with where we are now,

or how we got here?
Should I start with Iris,
with me,
or with Derek?
Where Iris was born?
Where I was born?
Where she found me?
Why she needed me?

I've learnt a lot about writing from Iris.
I've learnt it can be hard to know
where a story starts.

You might take false paths
and many re-drafts
to get to the right place.

You might start somewhere
and realise the story
actually starts somewhere else.

Let's start with Iris.

But in case you are wondering …

`Where are we now,`
`the team of three?`

Right now it's June 1938
and Iris and I are in Tsingtao.
The Hermes, I'm not sure.
In a suitcase, on the way to England?
It's not often the three of us are parted,
but there were reasons.

Tsingtao – where is that?
Six months ago, I didn't know either.
Look at a map of China:
find the Yellow Sea, trace the eastern coast,
halfway between Shanghai and Peking.

Aren't those magical names already?
Tsingtao.
The Yellow Sea.
Shanghai.
Peking.
So strange,
so far from home.

For the last two months,
Iris has been reported missing.
Missing on the front lines.
Missing in the field of battle.
Still missing.

We didn't know at the time
but she made headlines
around the world.

NZ GIRL'S TERRIFYING ORDEAL
WOMAN'S ADVENTURES IN BATTLE AREAS
Trek to Safety along Tsingtao Railway
TRAPPED IN CHINESE BATTLE ZONE
Lone White Woman's Trek
British Woman's Terrifying Trek
to Safety through War-Stricken China
NZ Woman Journalist in China

WAR ZONE PERILS
Amazing Story
GIRL'S AMAZING ADVENTURES ON CHINESE WAR FRONTS
A Woman's Experiences
HER REMARKABLE STORY: WOMAN MISSIONARY IN CHINA
Lonely Wanderings in Area of Conflict
AMAZING EXPERIENCES

These reporters didn't get all their facts straight.
(Iris, a reporter herself, would scoff in disapproval.)
Did they mean *woman* or *girl*? *New Zealand* or *British*?
And *woman missionary* she definitely is not,
although she did get help from one.

But *Amazing? Terrifying? Remarkable?*
That is Iris. That is what happened.
That is exactly right.

There is a war in China.
Tsingtao is under Japanese occupation.
The British consul and his wife,
Mr and Mrs Handley-Derry –
how strange is that name – welcomed us politely,
but I could tell they were shocked
at the state of Iris: her ragged clothes,
soles flapping on her shoes
and her bruised and battered body.
They ran her a hot bath,
burnt everything she was wearing,
gave her new clothes and shoes.
The amah mended her green coat.
The doctor checked her sore eye

and took out a thorn.
It was a relief to both of us
that she was not going blind, after all.

Honestly, I don't know how she survived
and to tell the truth
I'm relieved to find myself in one piece as well.

Mr and Mrs Handley-Derry
did not pay much attention to me.
People often don't.

How did we get here?

It's a long story.
Do you want to know?

We got here
by ship
by train
by ferry
by wallah-wallah
by rickshaw
by sampan
by donkey
by foot.
We got here
by air raids
by gunfire
by bombs falling
by tanks rumbling
by buildings crumbling.

We got here
by courage
by keeping going
by not giving in
by brushing off 'no'
by ignoring the men
who said a woman couldn't do it.

The same determination that powers her writing,
keeps her bashing away at her typewriter,
meeting deadlines, staring down rejections,
has powered Iris across oceans,
across continents, on endless train journeys,
along empty train tracks,
refusing to admit defeat.
That's how we got here.

Here is one beginning

For the first 18 years of my owner's life,
she didn't need me.
I'll tell you what I know of her life then.

Her name was Iris, her real name –
later, she had others.
Her birth certificate (perfectly beautiful,
written in Dutch, on vellum)
states that she was born in Cape Town
on 19 January 1906, to Nellie and George.
How did they end up in Cape Town?
George was born in Agra, India, also home
of the Taj Mahal.

Adelaide – Nellie for short – was on her way
from Australia to England,
but she never got there. The lure of travel
was already circulating in Iris's blood
when she was born.

Iris had an older sister, Hazel.
There would be two more:
Edna, and Ruth, the war baby.

See! Already you know about the
sisters (three).

The family sailed from South Africa on the *Ionic,*
Iris still a baby. Arrived in Wellington,
they lived in southern suburbs near the sea:
Melrose, Newtown, Berhampore,
under steep hills painted yellow
with flowering gorse and broom.
Russell Terrace, Waripori Street, Blythe Street:
close enough to hear the roar
of lions at the zoo: King Dick,
Briton, George, Mary and Maud,
echoing through the night;
close enough to climb on a tram
and trundle down to Island Bay,
where fishing boats bobbed on the tide
and Italian fishermen sold fresh fish
and baby octopus on the beach.

Iris can't swim for toffee, none of them can,
but I see her rescuing Edna, her sister,

who got out of her depth
and flung her skinny arms around Iris's neck
after she went out too far.

Or maybe Iris encouraged her to do that.

Because that's what Iris always did
went out   a bit
        too far.

That's what she always did.

Who is Iris?

I never knew Iris as a child,
I wish I had.
But this is how I picture her:
redhaired
adventurous
imaginative
curious
funny
smart.
Sometimes in trouble for scaring her sisters
with spooky stories in bed at night.
But even then, with a deep longing for beauty,
a love of green secret places.
and a heart for bright cheerful flower faces.
Named for a flower, after all.

She went to Wellington South Primary,
then Berhampore School, where the other kids

called her *brainy* – not quite a compliment.
In her last year, she was dux,
her name in gold letters on the honours board.

She went to Mr and Mrs Culford Bell's
Elocution and Dramatic Art classes.
I see her standing up to give a recitation
at their end-of-year concerts.
Words have always been important to her.

I see her with her sisters,
all four girls dressed in frocks
made on Nellie's whirring sewing machine,
the little Wilkinsons of Waripori Street,
and later (after welcoming their father
at the wharf, back from the war)
of 92 Northland Road, a house called Laloma.
The abode of love in Sāmoan, they're told. Maybe
not always. A house full of life all the same:
noise, quarrels and laughter. Far from the zoo,
no beaches here, but big skies and unexpected
glimpses of harbour down dense green valleys.
The house perched on a corner
above the road, overlooking bush and stream,
welcoming the wind streaming over the hills.

I see her climbing trees
exploring the bush
and riding horses
laughing at birthday parties
dancing with her sisters
as her father plays an old flute
that they have decorated with flowers.

I see her with two strong legs,
hopping, skipping, jumping,
flying kites,
her legs working just fine,
just like anyone else's.

How Iris became a poet

Here is one family story.

They were at the beach.
Iris was curled up in a small boat,
a dinghy hauled onto the sand,
while they searched for her
more and more frantically
along the tideline and in the sandhills.

'Where have you been?' they demanded
when they finally found her.
'I couldn't help it,' she said,
surprised by the urgency and fear in their eyes.
'I couldn't help it. I was writing a poem.'

That is another possible beginning.
The beginning of a poet.

When she was over the shock and the scolding,
Nellie bought her daughter an exercise book
to scribble her poems in.

I'm not making this up.
I've heard Iris talk about her childhood:
the Sunday school picnics,

the time she saved Edna from drowning,
the time her family lost her at the beach
and panicked,
but she was only writing a poem.

In 1919, she started at Wellington Girls' College
(navy-blue gym frock, white blouse, black stockings)
where she made friends-for-life with Gwen
of the long golden hair and green eyes.

That July, the country celebrated Peace Day.
At school, they sang *Land of Hope and Glory*
and the *Marseillaise*.
Miss Mary McLean, the lady principal, spoke of
the splendid work the nurses and women did in the war
and urged the girls to take up nursing as a profession.
The Bishop told them it rested with the young people
of today to bring about a better future. Most of this
would depend on women, so the girls should have
noble ideals, to bring in a better state of things.
Iris and Gwen rolled their eyes at each other.
They tended towards irreverence.

Iris was on the library committee and joined the
Rangiriri club for speeches and debates, Dramatic
Day and concerts. She won second prize in an essay
competition open to all the schools of the empire,
comparing the lives of Drake and Raleigh.

She was hailed as 'a schoolgirl poetess' in the newspaper,
her poems in the school magazine noted as
'some of the most striking poetry of the year'.

In her last year at high school, she had her first
poem in print, 'Flanders Poppies', published in
NZ Freelance on the day after Anzac Day.
Already she felt her poetry as a special, magic gift,
the only thing that was truly hers.

Where was I, all this time?
How do I know these things?
It's true I wasn't there.
But I've heard her talk about them
with Nellie, with her sisters, with Gwen.

I've heard her and Gwen talk about high school,
and the prizes she won for her poems and stories.
The money had to be spent on books,
but that was no hardship to Iris.
At Whitcombe & Tombs on Lambton Quay
she scanned the shelves
and picked out volumes of poetry,
Spenser and Keats and Omar Khayyam.

I've seen her and Gwen wiping their eyes with laughter.
'Remember,' Gwen hoots, 'that time when Miss McLean
told you to *take that self-satisfied look off your face*
and your name was read out at assembly –
all for going to the boys college sports day?'
Of course you couldn't ever be seen
talking to a boy while in school uniform.
Not even your brother (if you had one).

She left school. At 17,
she started work in a dusty newspaper office

with grey-haired older journalists,
30 shillings pay a week, some for lunches
and tram fares, some left over
for books and clothes
and hats.
The clatter of machinery
and the shout for deadlines
would be a soundtrack to her life.

Where was I?
Far away, far across the sea.
But soon, soon, our paths would cross.
Soon, this is where I came into it.
Soon, this is where her knee began to twinge.
Soon, this is where her life began to change.

Iris knows about hospitals

A hospital bed. That is another
possible beginning.

At 17, a swollen knee
seemed at first
a small thing.

Her knee was so painful
they sent her home from work
jogging along in a one-horse hansom cab,
each jog a little burst of agony.
The doctor, serious,
prescribed 'six weeks' bed rest'.
Rest wasn't easy to find

in that loving, tumultuous household
where arguments burst out of the walls
and resting didn't work anyway,
so Iris was sent to hospital
to lie on her back
as weeks and months slid by
in the real world outside.

Morphine.
A prick in the arm and the pain ebbed away,
breakers of peace rolled in like a king tide.
A fog of chloroform as the doctors operated.
A Thomas splint, like an iron cage,
to straighten and protect her leg.
More weeks in bed.
More morphine.
More sleepless nights.

The hospital was near the zoo.
At night the roars of the lions
caged, like her,
echoed through the empty streets,
until Iris hardly knew what was dream
and what was real
as her childhood receded
and the pain took over.

Other patients came and left.
Some never came out again.
Finally, hobbling in splints
and on crutches, she went home.

She still thought her knee
would get better, one day.

Of course, if it had,
I wouldn't be here
telling you this story

which is all true,

by the way.

By ship

How did we get here, to Tsingtao?
This is how it all started.
This is another beginning:
a wharf, a ship looming over us.

On Tuesday 18 January 1938
– just five months ago –
we climbed on board the *Awatea*,
Iris with her suitcases crammed with papers
her Hermes Baby typewriter,
her passport, some good walking shoes
and clothes thrown in at random.
I travel light. No luggage. Just me.
And I have no passport,
but this is what her one said about her:

Profession: Writer
Place and date of birth: Cape Town, South Africa.
19.1.1906
Residence: New Zealand

Height: 5 ft 6 ½ in
Colour of eyes: Blue
(I would have said *grey-blue, grey-green,*
the colour of the sea in all its moods.)
Colour of hair: Brown
(I would have said *amber.*)
Special peculiarities: Slightly lame.

Iris put away every penny she could
for months. She saved 150 pounds,
enough for a ticket to England.
That's what she was desperate to see:
English bluebells under English woods
in an English spring,
owls' nests and foxgloves
and English heather on English hills.

Most people go by boat. Not Iris.
She was taking the Trans-Siberian Railway,
a route so new and remote
it was like travelling to Mars.
Two and a half days sailing Auckland to Sydney,
a few weeks chugging up the Australian coast,
past Thursday Island and Manila
to Hong Kong. From there,
Japanese visa in hand, by ship to Kobe.

From Kobe to Vladivostok, Russia.
From Vladivostok to Moscow,
a fortnight by train, hard seat,
with an air cushion to soften the ride.

Such exotic, evocative-sounding stops.

A few days in Moscow, then Warsaw, Krakow,
Berlin and, at last, London.

That was the plan, but as Iris says,
'Chance is the lovely lord of any journey.'

Was it chance? Whatever it was,
The plan didn't work out that way.

Trains

Why? everyone asked. *Why the Trans-Siberian?*
But I know that Iris adores train travel.
The possibility of adventure
lurking around each bend.
The escape, for a length of train track,
from the real world.
The feeling of being no different
from anyone else. Sitting in a train seat,
no one can tell she has a limp.

Sometimes people trip over me
and Iris growls at them.
They are always very apologetic.

But most of the time on trains
she is surprisingly sociable.
I've seen her join in with impromptu singalongs
and once, on the way to Waitomo,
a treasure hunt through the carriages.
The 'treasure', some small treat

hidden in the pocket of a soft-toy wallaby
belonging to a rowdy party of Australians.

The *Railways Magazine* paid her two pounds ten shillings
for each article about her train trips.
(Iris said she would have done them for a pound
and still celebrated the amount.)
And she thought there might be more articles,
perhaps a whole book, in the Trans-Siberian Railway.

I saw the same things she did on our trips,
I always do,
but I'm in awe of the words she finds
to describe them.

She read the *Railways* articles out loud
as she bashed them out on the typewriter.
In Russell, she imagined ghostly masts
and sails of long-ago whaling ships,
ghostly prows of canoes
carving through the rippling waters,
ghostly figures in the graveyards.

In the Waipoua kauri forest, we followed a track
to Tāne Mahuta, old giant dripping
with kauri gum, holding up the sky.

Together we slept on lilos amongst the mānuka,
sat down to a breakfast spread of bacon,
currant scones, jam and tea
at a welcoming Māori house in Te Hāpua,
saw the glittering white sands at Parenga,
jolted over the rough road to Te Paki,

past rolling curves of sandhills to Spirits Bay,
past Māori gathering toheroa on Ninety Mile Beach,
where we got stuck, the car sinking into soupy sand,
rescued just before the creeping tide arrived.

We visited the glow-worm caves at Waitomo.
Explored Christchurch and Dunedin,
took the train to Queenstown,
steamer to Glenorchy and service car to Paradise.
We rolled across Foveaux Strait on the *Tamatea*
and hiked around Rakiura, Glowing Skies,
island of horse-drawn carts and only three cars,
where fat tūī drunk on honey tumbled out of trees,
bellbirds chimed and shining cuckoos trilled,
muttonbirds crooned in their burrows,
seals splashed among the rocks
and albatross soared through the sky.
We collected pāua and ambergris,
stalked kiwi with torches
under a sky blanketed with stars.

We caught the train to Arthur's Pass,
all dark bush, mountain streams and feathery waterfalls.
The trampers carried their alpenstocks on the train
and I felt part of a community,
even if they were snooty about their adventures.

We flew from Nelson to Wellington –
the only time we have been on an aeroplane.
Iris's mother was with us that time. Nellie, undaunted
by hurtling through the clouds,
couldn't see what all the fuss was about.

Iris and I have covered all three islands, north to south.
Together we have travelled by train and ferry
and service car, and once by air, but
she has seldom been out of the country.
She knew little of other places in the wide world,
but the idea of the Trans-Siberian didn't worry her,
any more than flying worried Nellie.

So there we were, on that Tuesday evening.
At 7 PM, the *Awatea* sailed for Sydney
with streamers and a band playing,
cheers and tears and arms waving madly
from deck to wharf, from wharf to deck.

Did I say *this is how it all started?*
This is not really how it started
because we had sailed on the *Awatea* before.
There was so much more
that happened
before this.

A farewell and a promise

A few days before the *Awatea* sailed
she met Derek, sat with him and said,
'I'll come back, when I have made my name,
and then we will find a house
where we can live together.'

A solemn nod.
Did he understand?
Derry was seven, now,

a sweet and capable age.
He could ride a bike, throw a ball.
A questioning age.
Here is a question he might have asked:
What do you mean, make a name?
Isn't it made when you are born?
But Derry didn't ask it.
He had grown up knowing
that Iris comes and goes.
Maybe he didn't realise how far
she was going
this time.

The other way

For a while, I wondered if
we might sail past my island.
It was mostly wishful thinking.
The islanders, laughing with excitement,
clambering up ladders, spilling over the decks
with their baskets of fruit and carved goods.
They would recognise me
and celebrate my return.
But now it seems we are going
the other way around the world
and I won't see my home again.
That tall rock rising from the ocean.
I won't hear the laughter
or the voices singing in farewell
as my people climb down the ladders
and into the boats and back to my island.

Sydney

We sailed across the Tasman Sea
and under the arching shadow
of the harbour bridge. Newly built,
it was hardly started on our last trip.

Iris has been here twice before.
Once as a child, without me,
when Nellie took the little girls
to visit her parents on the farm.
And the other time …
the other time on the *Awatea* …
that's another story.

Who am I?

You won't know yet.
I'm not a relative.
Not adult
or child.

I'm not a dog
cat
any kind of animal.

Keep guessing.

No.
No.
No.

What am I like?
Loyal, for sure.

That's my number one characteristic.
Sometimes, I admit it, I trip people up on purpose
but I get annoyed if they ignore me
or treat me as if I'm not even there.
When they stub their ankles or shins
I think, ha! Serves you right.
I'm reliable, easy to look after, don't ask for much,
put up with a lot. I'm a good friend.
Sometimes I wish I could do more.

To Hong Kong

In Sydney, Iris had a happy reunion
with her old friend Kay,
and we visited the Japanese consul's office
to get her visa for Japan.
You will come back wiser than you went away,
they told her, as they stamped a purple flower
inside a purple circle in her passport.

Then we boarded the *Changte*
to sail north up the Australian coast.

Local reporters came to check the passenger list
for their society columns.
Iris had written those columns herself –
always offloaded onto the female reporters,
along with the voices whining on the telephone lines,
complaining their name was spelt wrong
or missed out entirely from some important event.
So many people care about these things.

But this time, Iris was a minor celebrity herself:
WOMAN WRITER WHO WILL CROSS SIBERIA.
(Hard to tell which was more of a novelty:
Woman Writer or *Siberia.*)

Another Iris, 14 years old,
was going home to Hong Kong
after three years of Sydney schooling.
A bundle of mischief,
Little Iris giggled, gave Big Iris helpful advice
that might or might not be true.
There are tigers and bears on the streets,
she said. *A tiger pulled off a girl's arms*
and now she teaches with two sticks.
A bear ate a girl and a policeman, Little Iris declared.
If you are stopped by someone to exchange money with you,
you are powerless, you will be their servant forever.
Don't buy anything in the street, she warned.
Don't buy ice cream in the street,
or you'll go to the lavatory for six months!

The ship rolled a lot.
Iris wasn't seasick but
she needed me
at every step.

A stop at Brisbane.
Too rough to land at Cairns,
but Iris sent letters ashore.
On deck, too unsteady for the typewriter,
Iris scribbled away in a notebook
dotted with sea spray.

She was writing
writing
writing
all the time already
collecting impressions
like the seabirds that swooped
to catch food in the air.

The notebook

The notebook, I remember, was a gift
from her friend Ronald Holloway.
We waited in the Auckland sunshine,
Iris perched on a big rock, me leaning against it,
while Ronald went off to fetch some beer
and Iris christened the notebook with a poem
about the day, the notebook,
Ronald giving it to her and going for beer,
about the passers-by, sparrows, stray dogs,
about how she sits on the rock
like a lizard
but not so green
about the pink geranium growing next to it,
about how they drink the beer out of a jug
first emptying out the flowers,
nasturtiums, the colours of oranges and cinnamon.
Iris was never one for doing things
in an ordinary way.

The Hermes Baby typewriter

I remember getting the typewriter, too.

We bought it in January a year ago.
Iris and I made our way into town, to Queen's Arcade,
the British Typewriters and Office Equipment store,
where the Hermes Baby portable typewriter
sat on display, tiny but elegant
with its own carrying case.

The salesman was enthusiastic. He assured Iris
that despite its *amazingly low price*
it was *highly efficient!* 'Made in Switzerland!
Good Looks, Good Mechanism, and Good Typing
at a price within the reach of all,' he gushed.

What was this *amazingly low price*?
Twelve pounds.

Iris, my friend, is a writer.
She has published books, won competitions.
Once, out of an avalanche of 700 entries,
she won first prize in the *Sun* Christmas competition

for her short story, and second prize for her poem.
Ten guineas for one, three guineas for the other.
If only writing was always that well paid.

We were living in Wanganui
when *The Desolate Star* was published.
Her first book of poetry. Iris was so proud of it.
She scanned the papers for reviews:
a genuine poet … will be heard of very far away.
She left a copy carelessly lying on a table in her room,
watched sideways to see who picked it up.
When we were on our own, she caressed the cover,
leafed through the pages,
read out a poem here and there in a voice
that murmured and sang like the river outside.
I like all the poems. 'Hanmer woods' is my favourite,
and after that, 'Mists in the city'.
Both about places we have walked together.

When Iris puts something in words,
that's how you see it forever.
Autumn will run like a boy among the birch trees …
glory, in a shining sea of moonrise, lay on Lambton Quay.

She met a wild war veteran, Starkie for short,
and wrote his life story. She wrote one novel,
planned another called *The Godwits Fly*.
She read bits aloud, which is how
I learned more about her family stories.
She gave them different names, the Hannays,
but it was easy to tell who they were.

Easy to tell who Eliza Hannay was.
(Like me but very much pleasanter, Iris had decided.
And a sense of humour would be a help.)

She was elected to PEN, the writers' group –
an honour, you had to be invited to join.
Fifteen were invited. All but her were men.

Even if she was often called
Authoress
Poetess
as if *ess* means *less*,
the newspapers still praised her as *unusually versatile,*
and perhaps
the most individual writer this country has produced.

Surely there was money in this?
Yes, but not much.

'Am I a cuttlefish,' she yelled one evening,
'good only for squirting ink?'
She lifted the ink bottle,
ready to hurl it at the wall,
but the night nurse came in
and calmed her down.

Twelve pounds, an *amazingly low price*,
was barely affordable.

Iris lived frugally
but there was little money to spare.
She had dreams
and no money to make them happen.

Just as well my only food
is dirt and leaves,
and they come cheap.

But she bought the Hermes, and now
it's one of her most precious possessions.

We are a team, the three of us:
Iris, me and the Hermes.
The Hermes to help her write
and me to help her walk.

How I look at the world

This is how I look at the world.

I am close to rocks and dirt.
Sensitive to hard and soft surfaces.

This is how I keep my balance.
I scramble up hills,
stomp up steep flights of stairs.

This is how I go down hills,
bracing against ramps and slippery slopes.

This is how I hold steady and firm.
I am all about support.

This is how my shadow is straight and narrow
and sometimes stretches long and thin, like an arrow.

Who am I? Have you guessed yet?
I don't know how old I am.

Not very young
not very old
strong
reliable
upright.
I never put a foot wrong.
That's me.

Anything can happen

From Cairns, we sailed to Thursday Island,
off the far north tip of Queensland.

Leaves swayed in the breeze
on almond trees and coconut palms,
and flame trees blazed scarlet under the hot sun
alongside the startling bird of paradise
and starry frangipani flowers.

Coconut palms! How long since I had seen them!
I heard someone on deck mention Captain Bligh,
that he sailed past here after the mutiny
and named it after the day when he first saw it,
just as he named Sunday Island and Wednesday Island.
Iris was intrigued. We have a sort of connection
with Captain Bligh.

Little shops under verandahs lined the main street.
We went to the post office to post her mail, then
(because Iris wanted to see everything)
to a coral shop, and a pearl merchant's store,
where she tried on a diving suit and weighted boots.

Boats bobbing on the sparkling water
belonged to the Japanese pearl divers
who braved deep water, sharks and giant clams
to bring up pearl shells, later made into
buttons, jewellery and knife handles.
Many of the divers never went home again.
The sea got them, or sharks did, or the bends.
They stayed here, buried in the cemetery
under concrete or wooden posts
inscribed with Japanese characters.

There were many different nationalities
on this small island: Chinese, Torres Strait Islanders,
Aborigines, Malaysians,
Filipinos, Indians and a few others.
And Japanese, of course.
Old Japanese men sat out on deck chairs
in the cool of the evening.
The Boys on board the *Changte*
watched them warily.
We listened for the old Japanese ghosts talking
but there were none, unless they spoke
in the flutter of fireflies
or the deep booming of the locusts.

If you eat the wongai fruit –
plump and purplish-red, something between
date and plum –
you will come back to the island for sure.
That's what they say.
Little Iris bought a custard apple.

She and Iris waited for it to ripen and ate it
together, sweet and creamy and full of pips.
But wongai were out of season.
We will never go back.

Setting sail again:
sunset after spectacular sunset
tinged the wide sea orange and gold.

The stars wheeling above us slowly changed
as we crossed the Equator
and lost the Southern Cross.
New stars twinkled over our heads.

The temperature crept up and up
and up, until even the posh
saloon-class passengers were dripping sweat
in the tropical heat.

A strange smell got worse and worse.
Something tropical, we guessed,
until we found out what was in the *Changte*'s hold:
a full load of onions.

We passed through the Celebes Sea, dotted with islands.
Second class didn't get invited to Captain's Party night
but a stewardess snaffled us some treats.
Iris drank most of the iced beer.
Little Iris ate most of the cherry sundae.
We watched the lights of the Philippines slide past,
glowing red against the dark backdrop of mountains.

Look, birds! called Little Iris in excitement,
pointing down from the deck-rail.
Not birds but flying fish,
bowling along through the waves
like fast silver dragonflies.

Shark! Shark! the Boys called.
The sea was full of surprises
and danger.

The Boys

February the fourth was Chinese New Year
and the Boys let off firecrackers.
Boy Number One.
Boy Number Two.
Their sandals slap-slapped as they walked around.
At night they slept up on deck under a sky full of stars.
The Boys did not all understand each other –
they came from different parts of China
and spoke different dialects.
Not Boys at all, many of them,
but grown men with families of their own
to support from their meagre wages,
families whom they hardly ever saw
except for a few hours in port.
Boy Number One was a grizzled old man.
Boy Number Two was fat and seventy.
Still, known on board as Boy.

Manila

Then, Manila, capital of the Philippines.
Asia! A whole new continent!
Early morning, the boat's rocking stopped.
The deck echoed with footsteps and singing voices
as the cargo workers came on board,
busy unloading.
There go the smelly onions,
thank goodness.

Iris needed a shore pass to leave the boat
but it was too slow in appearing.
She marched down the gangplank anyway
without her passport, without permission,
braving the warnings about pickpockets.

Together, we took our first steps on Asian soil.
Together, we marvelled at
the *carretalas* – bright painted pony carts,
the shops selling snakeskin shoes and straw hats,
and stalls of embroidered blouses and scarves.
The stall keepers pounced on her, pulling her
towards their wares, clinging to her
like barnacles, and I had to ward them off
because I knew that arm was sore from her jabs:
cholera, smallpox and typhoid,
all raging in Hong Kong and further north.

Her arm was so sore, she could hardly lift it to do her hair.
Getting sick. Another thing I don't have to worry about.

She bought a spray of orchids, and a blouse,
and the stall keeper cried, 'You buy another!'
But Iris was hot and tired
and we returned to the ship.

By now, we were the only
second-class European passengers.
Iris had vowed to try everything.
She tried to learn Chinese phrases from Little Iris.
She tried to learn how to hold chopsticks.
She tried all the Chinese food:
bowls of rice heaped up like little white mountains,
soup, seaweed, sweet and sour pork,
red bean curd, bamboo tips, green onion,
roasted parsnip, preserved eggs with crimson yolks,
dishes of sauces and pickles,
and to finish, small delicious apricots
and glasses of China tea.

The Boys hovered, ready to pick up even a grain of rice
that fell to the floor.

Each day, a stewardess read out the news
from the radio bulletins for the Boys,
who couldn't read it themselves.
The crew, all Chinese, talked it over into the night,
their voices rising and falling in urgency.
Someone's village had been bombed.
'But we can still fight!' they said.
Once a Japanese ship slid past, very close.
The angry crew wanted to hurl things at it
and were upset, because they were not allowed.

Of course, Iris knew there was a war on.
Newspaper boys hollered the headlines
on Queen Street, before we left:
JAPAN GOES TO WAR, CHINA DEFIES JAPAN,
STRUGGLE IN CHINA, WAR CLOUDS IN THE EAST.

But now, the war
that had felt far away
started to feel closer.

Big painted Union Jacks appeared on our ship's sides.
'Anything can happen in the China Sea,'
warned the Chief Engineer.

How we first reached Hong Kong

Mist hung over the hills like wet white lace.

Curtains of rain swept over the harbour, but
I never mind the rain; it reminds me
of my island; perhaps it reminds Iris
of home as well.

The *Changte* moored in the harbour
and a small boat called a wallah-wallah
brought us to shore.

Iris cried when we said goodbye to Little Iris,
the stewardess and the Boys.
The *Changte* had been home for two weeks
and they were kind to us.

At the shipping office,
they said the *President McKinley* was delayed.

We were meant to go on board that day
and head straight to Kobe,
but instead we found a hotel,
the Metropole, in Repulse Bay.

Hong Kong was
busy
hot
steamy
noisy
dirty
exhilarating
different from anywhere we had ever been.
The harbour crammed with passenger liners,
cargo ships, tiny wobbly sampans and
red-sailed junks. The streets jammed
with cars, bicycles and rickshaws.
The pavements crowded with beggars
and little shoeshine boys.

Iris gave money to the beggars
and I worried she shouldn't
because she never had enough.

The language swung and sang in our ears.
Its script climbed like spiky twigs
over posters, signs and shopfronts.
Iris, enchanted, practised Chinese words.
She wanted to go everywhere, see everything.
We pounded pavements, peered in at shops
and workshops,
rode the funicular to the top of the hill,

where the whole astonishing city
was laid out below us
like a banquet.
At the top, Iris couldn't ignore the penniless jobless
and paid for us to return by sedan chair.
A special treat for me.
No work to do,
no need to guide or lead or steer around obstacles.
I lay back in luxury,
watching this strange alien world go by.

Our ship for Kobe was still delayed
and that was excuse enough for Iris
to change plans. She wanted to see
more of Asia, more of China,
which would have been a good idea
if there wasn't a war on.

Not safe

The nights were full of beating drums,
exploding firecrackers,
frightening off the New Year devils.

On our very first night in Hong Kong,
a girl from Siam
invited us to come with her to the movies.
We sat and laughed at Mickey Mouse.
It was raining when we came out
and we sheltered under the green waterproof
hood stretched over our rickshaw. Suddenly:
'What's that?' Iris exclaimed.

Shapes on the pavements and
bundles lined up in doorways,
half-noticed at first in the darkness, but then
impossible not to see,
because they were everywhere,
slumped like shapeless bags of potatoes –
but heads stuck out of these bags,
rags and old sacks their only protection
against the rain and cold.
Every day, more war refugees arrived,
destitute, a human landslide
of despair and want.
At night they slept out, hundreds of them.
Iris was vaccinated against smallpox
(and typhoid, and cholera) but here,
it spread like morning mist in the air.
Every morning the police went around
and took away the limp bundles:
men,
women,
children,
who had died on the ground, in the rain.

It's not safe to go to China.
That's what everyone told her.
But Iris didn't listen.
She never listened to *not safe*
or *not sensible*
or *not possible for a woman.*

She cancelled her booking to Kobe
posted her papers and extra luggage to London,
and we went to China.

To Shanghai

On 17 February, we boarded the *Aramis*
in Hong Kong, set off through the China Sea,
where anything can happen,
up the Yangtze River, up the Huangpu River,
to Shanghai.
Iris was alone and nearly broke but not worrying
much.
It helped that on board she met kind Mr Chung,
a manager at Wing On's huge trading company,
who found her cheap board and lodging
and wouldn't let her pay too much for anything,
not even a packet of handkerchiefs at Wing On's store.
'Too much!' he cried. 'Too much!'

There was a war on.
There was a curfew.
Shanghai, the backyard of the war, was an occupied city,
Japanese soldiers on the streets,
although in the French Concession
and the International Settlement,
where the foreigners and expats lived,
life went on much the same as usual.

We moved in with a German woman, Anna Wong.
Iris was charmed by her new Chinese name,
Wei Iri, and by our address:

House 3, Perfection Lane,
165 Rue Tennant de Latour,
Shanghai, China.

Anna's Chinese husband was away
but there was a small rosy-cheeked boy,
cared for and spoiled by an old amah,
who thumped along in pointed slippers
over tiny bound feet.

Outside the foreigners' safe enclave,
the city was a huge silent wreck:
houses and buildings gutted,
roads destroyed, schools empty,
refugee camps bursting with women and children,
their villages smashed to pieces behind them
and gangs of starving thief-children roaming the streets.

There was not enough food.
If the junks tried to go to sea,
they were captured and burnt.
There was no fresh fish, only salt,
in the markets.

The hospitals were crowded
with armless and legless men,
soldiers far from their country homes.
People died on the streets
of starvation, smallpox, measles, cold.
Every morning, after every icy night,
scores of bodies were picked up
and put on corpse wagons.

Once we saw one going past,
most of the bodies under canvas
but one small boy, in pink padded pyjamas,
thrown on top like a rag doll.

It rained. We woke one day to the white light of snow.
We were warm enough inside, in Anna's house.
Iris curled up under a crimson eiderdown,
but outside the homeless poor froze to death.

Smallpox was here, too.
Kids got lost in the mazes of alleys
a few blocks from home
and disappeared,
kidnapped off the streets.
Some were rescued
and sat in Salvation Army homes
waiting for their families.
They were no longer lost
but not properly found.
Others stayed lost,
perhaps forever.

With the roads ruined,
and no trucks going to town,
the peasants heaved their sacks of rice
on their backs or in wheelbarrows.
Women hobbled on bound feet,
bent under loads of firewood and vegetables.
Small children carried bundles of sticks
and handfuls of twigs,
scraps of anything, for the hope of a few coins.

Once, I've heard,
when Iris was six,
a whale was blown ashore in a storm
and stranded on rocks in Lyall Bay.
Its massive bulk rolled around in the tides.
Hundreds of curious sightseers crammed onto trams
or motored or walked or cycled to see the dead giant.
People hacked off pieces of whalebone from its jaw
until the stench of blubber drove them away.
Finally it was cut up and carted to the meatworks,
where an iron harpoon embedded in its back
was proof that this majestic creature
was attacked by a Cook Strait whaling boat.

And now: here she is watching
a huge country
attacked
ransacked
helpless
hacked to pieces.

Iris, now as then, gazed wide-eyed
with wonder and awe, but also excitement:
how lucky was she to witness such a sight.

She drank it all in.
That's what writers do.

No money, looking for work

In Shanghai, Iris thought, she might pick up
a newspaper job,
but that was a crazy idea.

There were no jobs, and anyway
it wasn't safe; journalists and publishers
had been killed and some decapitated.
Bombs shattered the windows of the *Shanghai Post.*
The Japanese were censoring foreign mail.
It was a dangerous time for anyone speaking out
or trying to report the truth.

Whenever we went out,
the beggar children appeared from nowhere
with their bare feet and pitiful cries.
Missie-sah, me starve!
Me starve!

Iris didn't give money to the beggars anymore,
not even when small girls in ragged clothes
ran along beside our rickshaw.
There were too many beggars, not enough money
to give to them all.
'What to do,' she said under her breath.
Giving, not giving. Both were a nightmare.

There were no jobs. She tried.
She went round the newspaper offices and Reuters,
the overseas news agency, and rang up PEN.
But everywhere was a blank wall.

Then she met Rewi Alley,
a New Zealander like her,
but already Chinese in his heart, fluent in Mandarin,
in China for over ten years and now
working as a factory inspector in Shanghai.

And with a Wellington connection:
his younger brother Geoff married 'little Effie Jamieson',
their neighbour in Blythe Street,
whose father once took a family photo of them all.

Rewi Alley took Iris out in his car to see
the devastation of the villages
smashed temples and houses
the cotton crop unpicked
and rotting in the fields
the cotton mills destroyed.

He told her about the factories
where children worked 14-hour days
in the steaming heat,
where children lost their fingers
in dangerous, unguarded machines,
got lead poisoning from battery-making
or died in explosions or fires,
where children slept under the work benches
at night, with bedbugs and lice; the factories
children couldn't escape from,
guards posted at the door.

It was Rewi who introduced her to Anna Wong
and Rewi who introduced her to Mr Timperley,
correspondent for the *Manchester Guardian*.
She had sent all her papers to London
and had none of her work to show him
but she wrote an article about the peasants
bringing their paltry crops to market,
and he seemed to like it.

All the time
she was writing
writing
writing
letters home
her notebook
drafts of articles
some in pencil
some in pen.

Every night she dreamed vivid dreams of New Zealand
and her family and friends
but she was cut off from them all,
with no chance of getting mail
until she got to England.

She wanted to be in England, at peace, so she could write.
She longed to be back home,
sitting in the front garden of 92 Northland Road
or wandering along Wilton's creek.
She wished she had bought a rough patch of land
and put up a wooden shack for her and Derek to live in.
So little money.
So many longings.

Then, amazingly, she got an offer of work.
Mr Timperley had a fund for Chinese publicity,
including films and writing, and the fund
would pay for her fares and living expenses for a month
to write articles for the *Far Eastern Mirror,*
a new pro-Chinese newspaper in Hong Kong.
She could go to Canton, maybe even further north.
She might get the material to write a book as well.

To Canton

At the wharf, Anna gave Iris a jade brooch.
We sailed back to Hong Kong
on the *Kaiser-I-Hind* ('Empress of India').

A line down the middle of the dining tables
divided Indian and Chinese on one side,
English and European on the other.
Iris hated that.

Already, we had seen plenty.
Refugees. Bombed villages.
Lost children.
Ruined cities.
Iris could have stopped at this point
and gone on to England.
It's not safe to go to China,
that's what everyone said.
But Iris never listened to *not safe.*
She wanted to see the war close up.
It wasn't the armies she cared about,
but the people,
the villagers, women and children,
the refugees flowing in all directions,
all over China.

Still in Hong Kong, we took a brief trip to Macao
with James Bertram, another New Zealand writer
visiting China. Tall, charming and self-assured
in his thick fur coat. Iris knew him

a little. He once sent her a flower
from Katherine Mansfield's grave in France.
(Another old girl from the same school,
another writer who travelled a long way from home.)

Macao was a short boat trip away
through sheets of soft grey rain.
We passed wooden fishing junks crewed by barefoot sailors,
who turned the spokes of an iron wheel with their feet
to hoist the great crimson sails.
They call Macao *Little Portugal,*
so perhaps I can say we've been there, too,
if we are counting countries.
We visited the stone cathedral, its most famous sight,
or what remained of it, only the façade left standing
after a typhoon blew the rest of it down.
We took a taxi to a faded old mansion for dinner
and looked down over crooked houses and roofs to the sea.

It was almost a holiday,
but only for a day.
Iris had work to do.

We made our way to Canton by ferry and train.
The Japanese hadn't yet reached Canton
but there were daily bombing raids
and bomb craters near the train lines.
The line to Canton was bombed, regularly,
bombed earlier that week, killing 23 passengers.
Buildings smouldered by the tracks.

The air still smelt of smoke
and burning wood.

Best advice, in case of a raid,
was to jump out and hide in a ditch.
Easy, if you don't have a bad leg.

We arrived in Canton in a thunderstorm.
Another strange new city.
We had no map,
no knowledge of the language
and a bundle of unfamiliar currency.

We found a room in the Oi Kwan Hotel,
a wedge of a building, one of the tallest in the city,
newly opened the year before.
Outside, seven storeys down,
the din roared like a river in flood.
Car horns tooting, streetsellers calling their wares
from rows of small booths heaped with mandarins,
sweet chestnuts, pork pies, rice cakes,
sugar cane cut in short lengths to suck on.
Beside the wide main street
the real river flowed quietly,
reflecting the bright neon lights of street signs
and the oil lamps that lit the booths.
Sampans and small boats clicked and clattered
on the black water, and in the booths
the wooden abacuses clicked and clattered too.

Her luck held. Iris met a school friend, Eileen Pope,
now Mrs Reo Fortune, married to a professor.
The Fortunes lived at Lingnan University,

a sampan ride across the Pearl River,
and Eileen invited Iris to stay.

On the town side of Canton,
twisty little lanes behind the main street
housed tiny factories turning out teak furniture,
fans, pictures, jade and ivory.

On the Lingnan side of Canton,
the countryside spread out
a green carpet of rice fields
crisscrossed by grass or stone paths.
White sails of small boats
moved like a dream along
hidden water channels.
At each village, the clay ancestral gods
nestled in a niche of the village gates.
Incense sticks sparked at their feet.

This was Canton:
soldiers' marching songs and bugles
waking us up each morning.
The scream of air-raid sirens.
The thump of anti-aircraft guns
like a giant hand on the roof.
Japanese planes zooming overhead.
The thud of bombs dropping
in the distance.
A bomb crater in a nearby street.
Kids collecting handfuls
of anti-aircraft shrapnel for sale.
That was just another day in Canton.

What did Iris know about war?

A little, but not much.

Her father worked in the Post and Telegraph Department. On 11 May 1916, he enlisted: 23746 Sapper George Edward Wilkinson, NZ Army Postal Service (NZ Engineers) 1st NZ Expeditionary Force. Two weeks later he sailed off to war, leaving Nellie with newborn baby Ruth and three rumbustious older sisters. It was a safe war for him, a postal sorter in London and Codford, but he was far away, and gone for over two years.
The girls saved their pennies for Red Cross copper trails, held flower stalls for the Belgian Distress Fund, took part in patriotic concerts.
Iris wrote a poem:

Hush thee to sleep, O gentle babe of mine,
Hush thee to sleep, beneath the southern vine;
Hush thee to sleep, holy and defiled,
Hush thee to sleep, thou art a soldier's child.

Nellie cried when her brother Bertie
was killed at Gallipoli.

The armistice and the influenza epidemic
went hand in hand.
Schools were closed, exams cancelled.
Nellie was a volunteer nurse;
she laid out bodies
in the houses of the dead.

Friday 8 November 1918:
Rumours swirled that the war was over at last.
Iris didn't hear them.
In bed with influenza, her head spinning and throbbing
she couldn't tell if the bells were ringing
in the churches or in her head.
Luckily, she only had a mild dose.
And on Monday 11 November,
Armistice Day, the war was truly over.

An eye for beauty

Iris saw beauty everywhere.
Even at the Grey Lodge, she could name
all the flowers in the garden:
springtime freesias, cheerful ranunculus,
white narcissus, scarlet anemones,
bright blue spraxias, black-eyed susans,
pansies, wallflowers, orange lilies,
a wild and random profusion of colour.
We limped outside together.
Iris knelt, dug her fingers into the dirt.
Flowers bloomed under her hands.
If she had a home of her own,
this is what she would do.

'Always wherever you go,' she told Derek once,
'try to make a garden,
even if it is only as big as a pocket handkerchief
and even if the place where you make it
belongs to someone else.'

Iris saw beauty everywhere,
even in the middle of a war.
She loved each place of refuge
that we found: the hotel in Hong Kong,
Anna's house in Shanghai,
and here in Canton, the tiled roofs
with their curves and peaks
glittering green and blue in the sunshine.
Even a bunk in a crowded train carriage
could be a temporary home.

Spring was arriving. Trees shimmered
with pink blossom and sun glinted on rice fields.
Sweet-smelling camphor trees, little orange trees,
rosy-leaved lychee trees.
In the villages where Chinese soldiers were billeted,
women spun cotton inside their houses
or worked bent over in the fields
– all the men gone to war –
and children stared with wide eyes,
toting babies on their backs,
sticks of sugar cane clutched in small grubby hands.
Wisteria, jasmine and honeysuckle twined
among the banyan trees. I always like to look
at things that support other things.
Water buffaloes wallowed,
ducks and ducklings paddled,
dogs barked, great fat pigs waddled,
chickens squawked in their coops,
frogs croaked in water-lily ponds,

butterflies flicked fragile wings.
But there was still a war on.

A gift for getting help

Iris had a gift for meeting people
who could help her,
or perhaps it was her bravery
and grit that they responded to.
They saw her limping doggedly
into their office, shop or hotel
and wondered,
what else is this woman capable of?
There was a war on, but
they signed papers for her
and issued travel passes
to let her continue.

There was a war on.
A bomb fell in the middle of Canton,
perhaps by accident, but that was no comfort
for the women and girls buried alive
or burnt to death in the sewing factory.
Red Cross members tore the rubble apart
with their bare hands, looking for survivors.
A thousand factory workers. One hundred and fifty died.

There was a war on, but
Iris had a free train pass to Hankow,
and a visa stamped into her passport.

What was she thinking?

She was thinking she wanted to go to the front.
She'd do anything to make it happen.
She knocked on doors,
begged, cajoled, met people
who sent her to other people,
who sent her to other people.
She was so determined.

The visa was not everything she wanted.
Sternly it announced:
'Bearer is strictly prohibited
to go to military zones,
fortified areas and unsafe places.'
But Iris wouldn't stop.
She wanted to get all the way
to the front.

When the railway lines were bombed
and the buses and trucks couldn't get past
the bomb craters in the road,
Iris always found a way
to go on.

Who am I?

Well, I have to tell you sometime.
Where was I while Iris was growing up?
How did I come into her life?

First, I was raised in another country,
far, far away. A dot in the ocean.
A tall rock like a fortress,
rising from the wide empty sea.

I lived among friends in groves of trees
swept by ocean breezes.
I could move by myself like a dancer,
feathery plumes swaying in the wind.
I felt myself growing taller
and stronger among my companions.
Fed by sun and rain
and freshwater streams,
we stretched our roots down into the ground.
We did not use the word *home*,
because we thought our island was the whole world,
surrounded by endless blue.

There were not many people on my island
but sometimes they came and walked among us,
laid their hands on our trunks,
inspected us with careful eyes.
Lifted knives.
Swung axes.

Then we were cut down,
taken away, shaped and moulded,
some into wooden boxes and bowls,
some, like me, into walking sticks.

`Did you guess?`
`That's what I am.`

I have mixed ancestry, now:
coconut, miro, orange wood.
You can tell because the grains are different,
darker, lighter or speckled.
Most of me, my long leg and foot,
is coconut palm wood.
The top end that Iris holds is miro,
and the two bands that circle me
between head and foot
are orange wood.

I was happy in the coconut and orange groves.
I didn't want to change into this new, stiff body,
my dancing days done,
my one foot unable to stand on its own.

There were not many people on my island
but sometimes ships would pass by.

The rock walls were too sheer for easy anchorage,
but the ship horns echoed across the water
and our island people paddled out
with their wares to sell.

Many horns had sounded
and ships passed by
before my carver was finished with me.
He sanded, smoothed, polished,
until I gleamed like warm sunlight, like
stars floating on water.

A ship approached, its horn rang out
and at last it was my turn.
My carver burst into the workshop,
grabbed a bundle of us from a shelf
and slung us over his back.

It was the middle of the night,
but the island timetable was ruled by the ocean liners.

Whoops of excitement,
men, women, children piling into small boats,
pulling on the oars,
rocking perilously on ocean waves in the dark.
The ship towered above us like a mountain.
Each boat moored by a rope ladder.
Feet swarmed up ladders onto the deck.

It was an adventure, for sure.
Did I want an adventure?
That, I didn't know.

My carver shimmied up the ladder with
baskets of fruit in one hand,
carved coconut shells in the other,
strings of shell necklaces around his neck
and us on his back.

'One hour, you have one hour,'
said a man in uniform.

Passengers crowded around us,
gawping at the profusion of fruit:
bananas, pawpaws, limes, oranges and pineapple.
For all my life I had taken these fruits for granted.
Who knew they were such treasures?

Hands ripped bananas, tore the peel off oranges.
Pineapple juice dripped over the deck.
Never tasted such sweet oranges!
voices exclaimed in wonder.

We slid around on my carver's back
as money changed hands,
or if not money, then hats, dresses,
scissors, handbags, jewellery
or any other items of impromptu trade.

'I'd like these,' said another voice.
My carver wriggled and shrugged us off his back,
laid us on the swaying deck,
and we changed hands
and left our home,
just like that.

The ship's bell rang.
Our people collected their unsold goods
and disappeared over the side,
back down the rope ladders.

As their small boats unmoored and sailed away
over moonlit seas, we heard
their voices singing familiar hymns,
fading away into the distance.

That was how I learnt the meaning of *home*.

I have never been back there.

There was a long journey.
A new country, a big city, a bustling port,
trams, crowded streets.
There was a shop.
We were stacked and propped on shelves and walls,
and one by one my companions left
until I was the last one,
and I thought I might stay there forever,
slumped, forgotten, masked under spiders' webs
and a thin coating of dust.

I dreamed of bananas, pawpaws, limes,
oranges and pineapple.

Vertical
is how I see the world best.
When I'm vertical,
I know I can help.
When I'm horizontal

it means I've been dropped,
thrown aside, kicked out of the way.
I'm no use to anyone.

I wished the carver had never found me
or had passed me by, judging me
weak or twisted or inadequate.
I thought: is this my final resting place,
this dark quiet shop?
I thought: do we get one big adventure in our lives
and I have had mine?
I thought: is this the end of my life?
But it was only the beginning.

One day, the bell rang
and the shop door swung open.
There was a hand picking me up,
swinging me round.
There was a firm voice saying, 'This one
is a good height.'

'All the way from Pitcairn Island,'
said the voice behind the counter.

That was when I heard the name of my home
for the first time. Pitcairn.
Pitcairn Island.

'All the way from Pitcairn Island.
Quite the traveller.'

'Then we will suit each other,'
said the voice over my head.

'I am a traveller, too.
We will travel together.'

And there we were, walking out of the shop.

And that's what we've done,
travelled together
ever since.

Anyway, that's my story,
but
this story isn't about me.
It's about my owner,
Iris.

I call her *owner*
but I think I am also her friend.
Her travelling companion,
confidant,
literal prop and support.
I am her protection and
her protector.

I am the one who goes ahead
at every step,
clearing the way,
making it safe.

In the Waipoua kauri forest, I remember how
we followed a track
to Tāne Mahuta, I remember how
I felt at home there.

It made me think about my lineage,
my ancestry, the rings of my being,
a secret nestled in the heart of me.

The trees told me their names.
Kauri.
Mataī.
Rimu.
What is your name?
I did not have one name to tell them.
(Except for, sometimes, *that dratted stick.*)
How old are you?
I didn't know.
Where do you come from?
I tried to explain it
but I didn't have Iris's words.
The kauri kindly asked my ancestry.
In a small voice I answered
humbly, because
they towered so high above me:
my heritage was mixed.
Coconut, miro, orange wood.
Their leaves rustled.
They told me not to be ashamed of my heritage
and to claim it wherever I went,
to claim the vast Pacific Ocean that circled my island.

Once, one of Iris's friends recognised me.
Warwick Lawrence, his name was; he and Iris
often met up for coffee and a sandwich
at our favourite eating place,

Blake's Inn on Vulcan Lane.
'From Pitcairn,' he proclaimed,
and nicknamed me 'Captain Bligh from the Bounty'.
'Phooey to that!' Iris corrected him.
She said Captain Bligh never made it to Pitcairn.
It was Fletcher Christian, his crew
and some men and women from Tahiti.
She told him the whole story of the mutiny,
so then I knew who our people were.
Some say descendants of pirates and mutineers;
others, that they were adventurers,
mistreated by their captain,
clever navigators, far from home
and making a new home on my rock in the ocean.

I see plenty of other walking sticks.

War veterans missing a foot or an arm
hike up the stairs to the newspaper office on them,
selling bootlaces for a scant living.

Old men and women, bent over with the weight
of years, lean on theirs for support.

Younger men, smartly dressed,
swing past with stick and top hat
on the way to their busy work.

Blind people hold canes painted white
or tap tap tap them on the pavement.

Other people, even children, hobble along
the streets with a stick to help,
one leg fat, one thin, withered by polio.

The trampers and mountaineers at Arthur's Pass
wielded their alpenstocks, ready to conquer the bush.

In Northland, we saw walking sticks
made from the wood of the *Boyd*.

Plenty of walking sticks, but
ever since we walked out of that shop together,
I have looked out for one like me.

Sometimes I've thought I caught
a glimpse of one of my Pitcairn cousins,
across a busy street or
in a crowded café,
but we have never met.

To Hankow

After three weeks in Canton, we set off again,
another long train trip to Hankow.
It was early April.
The railway station was a chaos
of people, pigs, ducks, luggage,
but a porter steered us to
the bottom berth in a four-berth carriage,
our home for the next 600 miles,
with a Chinese couple and a railway inspector.

'Do men and women sleep in the same carriage
in your country?' asked the railway inspector.
'No,' Iris told him. Perhaps not here, either,
until the war came.

Rivers crawled like crocodiles, slithered
like yellow snakes across the wide plains.
We were a long way from the sea,
from any sea.
Land stretched to the distant horizon
as far as you could see,
like the sea seemed to stretch
from my hilltop perch
on my island.

We gazed out of the train windows
until darkness fell.
At night, fires dotted the hillsides.
Lit, the railway inspector said,
to keep the tigers away.

How far we have all travelled,
Captain Bligh, Fletcher Christian,
Iris and me.

Tea but no milk

There was tea but no milk or sugar.
The food on board ran out –
No porkie! No fishie!
And there was little to eat except
hard-boiled eggs
from station vendors.
Don't buy anything in the street,
Little Iris once warned,
or you'll go to the lavatory for six months!

When the train reached Wuchang,
the Chinese couple looked after us.
We crossed the wide sparkling Yangtze River
by ferry, under midnight moonlight
that shone ruby and pearl.

A tired rickshaw boy pedalled us to an all-night tea shop,
where they let us sleep in one room upstairs.
Iris curled up under her coat. I lay on the floor.
In the morning, another rickshaw boy took us
to the British Consulate.
We never saw the kind Chinese couple again.
That's what happens in war time.
People disappear.
I wonder what happened to them.

In Hankow, there were beggars everywhere,
Chinese soldiers everywhere.
The great Yangtze River flowed past, to Shanghai,
to the faraway sea.

Iris was allowed to attend the 5 PM press conferences.
Dr Li, Director of Chinese Intelligence and Publicity,
released each day's official bulletin from the front.
Pins on maps traced battle lines
and troop movements. Afterwards they drank tea,
ate small cakes and Chinese sweets.
She was the only woman there,
but she still hadn't seen what she wanted to.

Hankow was not far enough for Iris.
She wanted to go further.

To get to the front,
to the *military zones* and *unsafe places*,
you needed an official pass.
Iris kept asking, but they wouldn't give her one.
Nobody would help.

In Hankow, we stayed at the Lutheran Mission
with Edith Epstein, who taught English
to big Russian pilots.
The pilots had come to help fight the Japanese.
The war had been going badly
but the Chinese had just won a great victory
at the front, in a place called Taierhchwang.
Edith's husband, Eppy, had scored a great scoop,
the only reporter on the scene.

After Taierhchwang
there was a special press conference.
We crossed the Yangtze River back to Wuchang,
where two generals reported on the great victory
and interpreters followed up in English.

Eppy was still touring the battlefields.
We went out with Edith
to eat at a French café,
past the Chinese sentries standing in the streets
ready to warn us to take cover
if there was an air raid,
because it was the week of the full moon
and that's when the bombers flew.

There was an air raid,
but we were safely inside.
Iris and Edith ate dinner in the dark.
From the windows we watched
tall buildings turn black
as lights switched off.
The clamour in the streets
died down. Pony carts and cars
moved to shelter. The rickshaw boys,
who had no shelter, sank down
between the shafts of their rickshaws.

We saw the Japanese planes
silhouetted by moonlight, silver and gold
where the searchlights pinned them
against the clouds.

When Eppy came back, he listened
as Iris declared, 'I want to see the front.
I want to travel on foot with the refugees.
I want to see the war, not as a chess game
of two opposing armies
but as a *real* crisis that affects *real* people.'

Eppy saw beyond her stiff leg
and me. He saw her passion, her determination,
and he was a war reporter, so he understood.
He invited her to a film-showing
about the battle at Taierhchwang.
Iris was asked to make a speech.

She had nothing prepared, her eyes were bunged up
and sticky with dust, there were hundreds

of other eyes on her,
but she did it. I was so proud. She talked about
the big and little countries of the Pacific,
how they also wished for the peace of the world,
how China was fighting for all of us.

Was it Eppy's help, or her speech,
which got reported in the Chinese papers,
or her persistent knocking on doors?
Was it her New Zealand passport?
Whatever it was, at last she had
what she wanted, a pass to Hsuchow
in English and Mandarin
with a red seal and lines of Chinese script
in which the words 'Robin Hyde'
climbed vertically down the page
and a request, or order, to 'whom it may concern
to give Bearer such assistance as they properly can'.

Iris was thrilled as a small boy
with an unexpected armful of toffee apples.
She never thought she could pull it off.

She was homesick for New Zealand.
She missed her family.
She worried about Derek.
But every bit of China fascinated her.
She wrote to her father that it had already been
the most wonderful trip in the world.

It was April and we were meant to be in London
but here we were, still in China

and no sign of leaving.
Iris was official now,
officially on the way to the front.
She was getting her wish.

To Hsuchow

Iris left most of her luggage behind,
even her beloved Hermes Baby portable.
Dressed in slacks and shirt, walking shoes,
brown silk hat and heavy green coat,
all she took was a small case,
a blanket and me.
We boarded another train to Hsuchow,
gazed out grimy windows at small villages
and a big walled town,
stone towers and mud brick walls,
wheat fields, pagodas and crumbling fortresses.
Peanuts and pastries for sale at each small station.
The fans didn't work, the toilets were filthy, blocked
and crawling with flies. It was hot and stuffy.
A train passed us in the other direction
crowded from steps to roof
with fleeing refugees.

We shared a carriage with a Chinese girl.
She and Iris shared smiles,
cups of tea, but no language.

At midnight we reached Chengchow.
The station was in darkness,
the ground studded with black mounds

of weary soldiers sleeping on their packs.
The Hsuchow Express was waiting
on a different platform.
We ran/hopped/hobbled –
Iris, me and the Chinese girl –
but every doorway was blocked
and bulging with passengers.

'Lift me up!' Iris yelled to a tall Chinese soldier
who knew no English but understood her urgent gestures
and hoisted us up, one by one –
Iris, me and the Chinese girl –
head first through an open window.
It could have been a disaster for her bad leg
but we landed on top of the soft squealing mass
of a pig tied up in string mesh.
The pig shrieked louder than any of us.

Soldiers already crammed into bunks
made room for us –
bottom bunks for Iris and the Chinese girl,
each shared with a soldier.
More soldiers on the top bunks and on the floor.
No time for modesty here.
There was a war on. Nobody cared.

One Chinese boy who spoke
a little English tried to explain
that we would reach Hsuchow by morning.
Iris and the Chinese girl sang songs for the soldiers
through the night,
but in the morning, we were not at Hsuchow.

We were at a small village called Liu Ho
and here we sat
and sat and sat.
We sat here for two days,
while up ahead railway gangs toiled
to fix the lines, blown to bits
by a bombing raid, like the 200 people
nearby at the time.

We sat here for two days
sweltering in the heat, choking on dust, swatting flies.
Beggars wailed at windows and doors,
holding up babies dressed in rags.
The Chinese boy who spoke a little English
translated their cries for Iris,
but the words hardly needed translating.

Have a kind heart.
Give money.
Do kindness! Do kindness!
No food.
Take pity on the baby.
Give money.
Have a kind heart.

This was bandit country.
It wasn't safe to go far from the station.

But a few times, there were air raids
and we all left the train,
trudged over wheat fields,
found shelter under trees or in dugouts
with the old ladies and babies of the nearby villages.

There was no food on the train
but the station master took pity on us,
invited Iris in
and fed her on slippery fried eggs and toast.

Trains of wounded soldiers went past,
bandaged and staring blankly
at nothing.

It was hard to know what was happening, except that
our train was going nowhere,
but the Chinese girl and two soldiers looked after us.
When a troop train arrived,
they grabbed their belongings
and beckoned us to come with them,
scrambling up the tall steps
like climbing a ladder.
An officer wanted Iris to get off
but her pass worked its magic
and he let us stay.

The train didn't stop at Hsuchow, so we had to jump off
as it slowed down. Another potential disaster,
but Iris didn't hesitate.
She dropped her case, coat and me,
dropped
herself

onto the sand.

The soldiers carried her luggage through the streets,
past watchtower and pagoda, small clay cottages,
yards dotted with squawking poultry

little shops selling rolls of colourful cottons,
factories making pottery, brass bowls
and silk umbrellas, birds in cages,
street vegetable stalls and peanut sellers,
to the China Travel Service hotel.
Mules trotted past, bells jingling
on their scarlet saddles.
Rickshaws decorated with painted butterflies
rattled over the cobbles,
their drivers gawking in surprise
at our small procession.
There were gaps like missing teeth in the walls
and the front doors of the hotel were boarded up.
The war was not here yet,
but it was close.
It was coming.

The girl, our train-friend,
was here to meet her soldier husband.

I wonder what happened to them.

Not far enough

Even Hsuchow was not far enough for Iris.
She wanted to go further,
always.

Four reporters were already here,
one Chinese and three European.
All men, cameras casually slung round their necks,
but they didn't want her company.

They said she would hold them back.
Being lame, they meant.
Being a woman
and lame.
They thought women
were only good for looking beautiful
and rocking the cradle at home.
But I think
she would have helped them
more than they could ever help her.

Dr Nettie

In Hsuchow we met Dr Nettie Grier,
American, 70 years old, now widowed.
She'd lived here for nearly 40 years,
spoke fluent Mandarin,
dressed like a Chinese woman,
a doctor at the Mission Hospital
and refused to desert her post
even as the Japanese were advancing.
The mission had two hospitals,
one under Dr McFayden for men,
one under Nettie for women and children,
already full of bombing cases,
burns and bullets.

Dr Nettie asked Iris to stay.
There was real American food,
coffee and cookies and cherries.
Iris fell asleep in a lavender-scented bed
and hardly stirred for hours.

Nettie was used to doing things
that people told her she couldn't do.
When Iris said she wanted to go to the front,
Nettie didn't say, 'You can't do that.'
She found a way to do it,
but for this Iris needed yet another pass
from the Most Official of Officials.
'Go to the general,' Eppy had instructed.
Iris ignored that advice, in case the general said no.
But she visited the general's secretary
and collected another pass and red seal.

On the *Wanganui Chronicle*, Iris often wrote
about all the things that women couldn't do.
Women in Parliament were only there
to clean and tidy up,
and there were still no women MPs.
Women in hospitals were only there
to nurse or be nursed,
and there were few women doctors.

Later, she wrote about some of the things
that women dared to do:
drive cars, fly aeroplanes
learn the new dance steps
have their hair shingled or bobbed
wear backless swimming costumes.

Now Iris was joining them
by daring to do the things
that women weren't supposed to do.

That evening, we went to the East Railway Station
and got aboard a train for Yun Ho,
the end of the line, and
nearest station to the front.

They put us in the cook's compartment.
At midnight we reached Yun Ho.
Soldiers took us downstairs into a concrete dugout,
where officers were talking on field telephones.
They brought fried eggs on toast for Iris
and found her a bed for the night.
I lay beside her.

In the morning
we saw donkeys plodding around grindstones,
a peaceful sight, while in the distance
we heard the guns roaring.

They took us to a big house,
served fresh bread for breakfast,
showed her their battle trophies:
banners and swords and guns,
letters and diaries and photographs,
and let her take her pick.
Iris chose a silk banner of the Rising Sun,
marked with Japanese characters.

She had got what she wanted.
Now we were going to the front.

We piled into a truck and set off with
two overseas Chinese reporters
and Paul, the interpreter.

We passed the other reporters, coming back.
Their astonished faces
as the trucks passed each other
were a sight to behold.

Then the Japanese bombing planes arrived.
It was hard for Iris to struggle out of the truck.
Even with me helping, she was the last one out
and everyone else had melted into the fields.
When Paul found her, he showed her
how to use the green wheat ears
as a hood, for camouflage,
because we could be here for hours
while the Japanese planes circled above.
They were looking for villages
that might be billeting Chinese soldiers
or sometimes they just bombed them
anyway, like now:
the screaming dive
the quake and thud of a bomb dropped
and the planes disappearing into the distance.

We climbed back into the truck.

Only two women would ever get this far:
a young Chinese reporter, Chang Yi-lien,
and Iris.

The basketmaker's hut

We went past the walled town of Pihsien,
and then, on foot, to a small village

all made of wood or stone
or clay or straw, just one ordinary village
among thousands, nothing special.

In a small hut, the general's headquarters,
they served up dinner: soup and vegetables.

We stayed the night by candlelight
in the village basketmaker's hut.
Bats fluttered in the courtyard
and pomegranate flowers glowed red
under a new moon.

All night the guns rumbled.

In the morning curious children peeked around the door.
The bravest came closer to touch her.
Iris gave them a few dollars, the only gift she had,
but nobody seemed to know what to do with the money.
Paul translated the children's names:

Little Horse
Field
Plough
Spade
Miss-Flower-That-We-Eat
Small Moon.

And Iris couldn't help but think
about her darling Derry.

I couldn't help but notice
the bound feet of the women

so tiny
when I looked at my own one strong foot.

I wonder what happened to the women
and the children.

Her darling Derry

Derry? Derek?
Who is he?
Where is he?
Who is looking after him?
Isn't that what you're asking yourself?

It all goes back to
Wanganui.

Wanganui was
the shining river
flowing through the town
sweeping past the window of our room
swirling through our dreams.

I watched the way it slid round corners.
I envied its twists and turns,
its languid easy movement

but sometimes that's just how it is.
Some things are meant to slide and curve.
Some are meant to stay straight.

Wanganui was
the siren of the river steamer
shrieking in the early morning,
grey-misty cold floating off the water,
Māori women crouched on deck,
black shawls drawn over their heads,
clay pipes between their teeth,
greenstone around their necks.
Canoes drawn up on the riverbanks.
Birds darting through the trees.
Still mirror pools reflecting overhanging ferns.
The hotel at Pipiriki, the mission station
and cherry orchard at Jerusalem.
Dark caves, glimpses of old pā sites.
Boys on horseback,
murmuring Māori voices.

Wanganui was
black swans sailing on Virginia Lake.

Wanganui was
a new job, lady editor on the *Wanganui Chronicle*
producing columns under a new name: Margot.
Writing up Boat Club dances, Rowing Club balls,
pantomimes, weddings, football matches,
the Bachelors' Ball at the woolshed,
the Fire Brigade Ball, the first garden party of the season,
bridge parties, race meetings, dress shops,
jewellery shops, shoe shops.
Recording who wore the pink taffeta,
who wore the apricot georgette with silver lace,
who wore the black satin and the Spanish shawl.

Wanganui was Henry Lawson Smith,
a war veteran: Gallipoli, France,
a fellow journalist,
married, with children.

Secrets

Iris has always been good at keeping secrets.
She got a doctor's certificate
for six months' sick leave 'for her heart',
but she would keep writing her Margot columns
for 25 shillings a week.
Henry Lawson Smith would pay a few expenses
but otherwise, she had no money.

Iris was good at keeping secrets.
Nobody knew, except Gwen and me
and Henry Lawson Smith.
Not her sisters,
not even her mother.

Gwen knew someone who knew somewhere
we could stay.
At sunset, we sailed from Wellington
on the *Tamahine.* At 3 AM,
a thump on the cabin door, a wake-up shout:
'French Pass in five minutes!'
Cold air, moonlit night,
dark glittering water, looming hills,
a jetty, a waiting man with a lantern,
who led the way to the silent hotel
and a bare room, lit by a candle.

We were on the way to D'Urville Island,
which has no hotel
but local families who put people up.
No one would know her here.

The island, a hunk of rock in the sea,
reminded me of my long-ago home.

Not a real Mrs

Iris had a fake wedding ring
and a fake name: Mrs Challis.

We were happy on the island,
wandering, exploring, clambering over rocks
as Iris's belly grew,
watching oystercatchers paddle and gannets dive.
Iris feasted on homemade bread, butter and jam.
But our hideaway didn't last –
some excuse made by our host family,
perhaps true, perhaps not.

We moved to Picton.
Iris's belly was swelling –
no hiding this baby now.
One more landlady threw us out
when she found mail addressed to Miss Wilkinson,
not a *Mrs* after all.

But at last we found safe haven,
with another landlady who didn't care,
and soon the baby would be here.

Iris was content, sewing baby clothes,
roaming from library to seafront,
writing her columns.
Peach trees were flowering.
The days drifted past like blossom.
The sea was peaceful.

Then the *Wanganui Chronicle* cancelled her contract.
No more Margot.
No work.
No pay.

A beautiful boy

Picton hospital. Hours and hours of agony.
In the end she screamed like a seagull
and the nurse tutted and scolded her,
'You've been so splendid till now!'
Being *splendid* means not screaming.
Women are meant to suffer childbirth
in *splendid* silence.
Suddenly, the room shook and trembled.
It was an earthquake, quite a respectable one,
and minutes later, the baby was born.
'You've got a boy, Mrs Challis,' the doctor told her.
A boy, alive and healthy,
with hair glowing reddish gold,
a beautiful boy. Names are important.
Iris named him Derek Arden Challis,
Derek because she liked the name,
Arden after the forest of Arden
in Shakespeare's *As You Like It*.

The governor-general and his wife
were touring the area.
Lady Bledisloe visited the hospital.
The mothers in the maternity ward
showed off their babies
and Lady Bledisloe admired them all.
There were no husbands to be seen,
so she didn't know
that Iris wasn't a real Mrs.

Iris didn't know much about babies.
She was awkward with Derek's bottles
and nappies, but when the nurses brought him
she stared at him, entranced,
for as long as she was allowed.

Two weeks later, we boarded the *Tamahine.*
Iris carried Derek hidden in a basket,
like a little blue-eyed doll.
In Wellington, she put him in a nursing home.
Every day, we went to visit him.
Only two weeks past childbirth,
Iris hid her exhaustion
the same way she hid everything.

Her workmates didn't know about Derek.
Her sisters didn't know.
Her father didn't know.
Even Nellie didn't know.
Iris was so good at keeping secrets.
But it wasn't just secrets she had to keep now.
She had to keep a baby,

and how could she do that
with no job? The nursing home was so expensive.
Her savings were leaching away.

Gwen invited us for Christmas. She was married now
(Iris was her bridesmaid), with a baby of her own.
Hawke's Bay was hot and sunny.
I watched Iris and the baby getting to know each other.
Day after day they spent together,
although in public he was called a nephew
to avoid gossip or secrets leaking out.
I watched Iris stoop over his cot,
gazing at his tiny fingers,
his cheek on the pillow,
listening to each quiet breath.

Gwen knew someone who knew someone.
Mrs Rattan, an Irish woman in Palmerston North,
could look after Derek for a pound a week.
Mrs Rattan knew, or guessed,
but she didn't mind or care
about the no-Mrs situation.

And then Iris was offered a job.
Lady editor at the *Observer*, four pounds a week.
The job was in Auckland, but
perhaps she could make this work after all.
Perhaps one day she could earn enough
for her and Derek to live together.

January 1931: a new start.
We moved into the Burwood Private Hotel
on Princes Street, near the university.

Harry Sweetman once stayed at the Burwood.
But Harry is dead and gone;
he will never come back.

Iris paid 30 shillings a week for board
and one pound went to Mrs Rattan,
who fed Derek condensed milk
but was kind and loving.
There wasn't much left over.

That was a long story,
but now you know about Derek.

You don't know about Harry, yet.

And you don't know what happened
last time, that *last time* we were in Sydney.

But that's enough for now.

Back to China.

By donkey

The general gave Iris a uniform:
pants, tunic and puttees,
and showed her how to tie them,
and we set off to the headquarters
of another general, three *li* away.
(A *li* is a Chinese measure of distance,
less than a mile, perhaps a third.)
The others were on horseback, but Iris
couldn't manage the stirrups with her bad leg,

so I swung behind her
as we rode on a donkey.

The headquarters were in a small house and courtyard.
(These were not generals who lived apart in luxury.)
There, we met another group
who had already been up the mountain
and among them was a woman,
Chang Yi-lien, elegant in a long blue gown,
the interpreter for the Russian reporter,
fluent in Russian, Chinese and English.

Nanshan Mountain was the front line.
Chinese on one side, Japanese on the other.
In this huge country, as vast as a whale,
racked by war, the dividing line
was right here in front of us.

Then we climbed the mountain.

They thought Iris couldn't manage it, but she did.
They thought she would turn back,
but she clung on to the donkey
as it scrambled up the steep slopes,
hooves clattering on scree and stones.

The same determination that keeps her bashing at her
typewriter, meeting deadlines, staring down rejections,
powers her writing, powered her up this mountain,
kept her battling her way uphill,
refusing to admit defeat.

Young Chinese soldiers in tin helmets
and thin cotton uniforms were reading or writing letters
or sleeping on mats in shallow rocky dugouts.
Some were guiding the swing of a big telescope
aimed at the villages below. They let her take a look,
mimed *Keep your head down!*

Guns boomed. Puffs of smoke
rose from the villages below us,
where figures dressed in white,
Japanese soldiers, looked small
and strangely ordinary.

This was it. This was 'the front'.
Iris had reached her goal at last.

What a long way we all were
from home: the Chinese soldiers,
the Japanese soldiers, Iris and me.

Back down the steep hill
in a sudden thunderstorm.
Back to the basketmaker's village.
Goodbye, little curious children.
Goodbye, tough and loyal donkey.
Back to the noisy, rattly trucks.

We set off back to Hsuchow
but now things had changed.
The roads were clogged with refugees,
peasants fleeing their homes
with carts and wheelbarrows
for their few belongings
and for the old women who couldn't walk

because of their bound feet.
We stayed overnight in the hut of yet another general,
who gave Iris a Japanese sword as a souvenir.

When the planes came again
I helped her out of the truck,
and we limped-stumbled-ran together
into the wheat fields, took cover
as the planes circled overhead
and villages burned in smoke and flames.

I tried to help her, but she didn't seem frightened.
We found ourselves sheltering with Chang Yi-lien
and the two women talked, and picked and ate wild peas
sprouting amongst the rows of wheat.
Chang Yi-lien said urgently:
'Tell the world what is happening here in China,'
and Iris promised that she would.

Back to the station at Yun Ho.
Paul, the interpreter, jumped off the truck,
not even time to say goodbye and thank you.
I wonder what happened to him.
I wonder what happened to

Little Horse
Field
Plough
Spade
Miss-Flower-That-We-Eat
Small Moon.

I wonder what happened to all of them.

The bombs start falling

A ferry took us across the Grand Canal.
At last we got back to Dr Nettie's compound
and then the bombs started falling.

For hours the planes swooped overhead,
so low we could see their markings.

The ground shook with thuds and bangs.
Fire rained down from the air,
fire flowered on the ground.
Houses were obliterated, and
the air filled with tears and weeping,
screams and wails.
Dr Nettie stayed calm and serene.
Even with no electricity,
she operated by candlelight.
Iris burnt her Chinese uniform
and buried the Japanese pennant and sword,
too dangerous to be found with them
when the invaders arrived.

Wheelbarrows and handcarts rattled over the cobbles
as people fled the town, carrying their possessions
tied up in bundles on their backs.
Rickshaws vanished off the streets.
Shutters went up on all the buildings.

The story of Harry

On 13 May, Iris looked at the date,
remembered another 13 May,
a departure and a death – many years before
but still an ache in her heart.

It started when a young man
stepped into her life
to change it forever.

Iris was 16, still at school,
when George brought home a fellow worker
from the post office. His name: Harry Sweetman,
five years older than her, from Te Uku, Raglan.
Harry Sweetman, a young man with big dreams.
He enchanted them all, and Iris enchanted him.

The very next day, he visited her at school.
Imagine, at school! The drama! The commotion!
The flushed cheeks of the girl who brought the message:
'There's a man to see you, Iris.'
The permission needed from the principal!
Harry gave her two books and a bundle of his poems.
He was leaving Wellington to work as a linesman
but they promised to write to each other.

Later, Harry moved to Auckland
as a car salesman for the Ford Motor Co.
The letters they wrote were pages long.
Iris stored her letters from him in an old cabin trunk.
I've seen her take them out,
carefully smooth them, reread them
time and again.

One Easter, Iris went to visit him,
all the way up the island by train.
It was two years since they had met.
They climbed a hill in the moonlight,
sat on the grass for a moonlit picnic.

What Iris didn't know
when they said goodbye:
she would never see him again.

October 1925. Harry Sweetman set off
on the *Waimana* to see the world.
He sent a telegram from the wharf:
'Off on the great adventure.'
New York, Boston, London.
Such enticing names.

Then, for months, there was nothing
from him. No letters. Not a word.
Iris waited and waited. Finally, hopefully,
she sent a telegram to his home at Te Uku.

Have you finished wandering, Ulysses?
If so write to 92 Northland Rd. Iris.

Almost at once a letter came back
with Harry's familiar handwriting on the envelope.
Iris tore it open, excited, relieved –
but it wasn't his after all.
The letter was from his brother Hardy.
Their handwriting was eerily similar.

This is what Hardy told her:
that Harry arrived in London in December 1925
that he got a job in Manchester
that he got tonsillitis
that he had an operation
that he got pneumonia
that he died on 13 May 1926.

When Iris got that letter
it was nearly Christmas 1927.

How could it be? Harry, in her head constantly
all that time, but gone from this world
for a year and a half, and she never knew?

Harry has been gone from this world
for 12 long years, now,
but still the ache is there.

Staring eyes, squirming maggots

Rows and rows of eyes
staring at us:
22 Chinese soldiers
lying in their beds
thirsty, filthy,
bandages black and sticky with flies.

The nurses, busy and deft,
did what they could with
no soap
no splints to set broken legs
no morphine for relief

no anti-tetanus serum
not enough clean bandages
not enough of anything:
a basket of dressings
a big iron kettle of boiling water
some dirty towels
and aprons.

Iris, shocked and shaken,
did what she could,
learned to vaccinate,
dress wounds, fold new lint pads,
helped to feed the refugees.
She eased off bandages and
used forceps to drag yards of packing
out of deep gaping wounds,
washed them out,
dabbed with iodine.

The patients grasped her hands and tried to talk
but the only words she had for them were English.

Good morning
I can't speak your language
I feel very sorry for you
Would you like a drink of water?
All right, all right.

The wounds were infested
with wriggling maggots.
Maggots crawled on the sheets.
Maggots fell onto the floor.

Stamp. Stamp.
Iris stood on them, twisting her shoes around.
Stomp. Stomp.
She thumped me down too.
Maggots under her feet.
Maggots under my foot.
Stamp. Stamp.
Stamp.

Chinese soldiers,
eyes unmoving in pain,
bravely trying to smile.
Nothing moving except the maggots
squirming
underfoot.

The city falls

The next day, 19 May, the Japanese arrived.
Iris, Dr Nettie and the frightened nurses
watched through cracks in the hospital gates.
Men on horseback, soldiers on foot, tanks,
more tanks, more foot soldiers.
The procession lasted for hours.
The city had fallen.

The next day,
the 22 soldiers were dead,
bayoneted where they lay,
with their brave eyes
and broken legs
and clean bandages,

those rows of unblinking, stoic,
suffering soldiers.

First bombs, then tanks

First, bombs in the air.
Then, tanks in the streets.

We were surrounded,
isolated, cut off.
There was no way out.

Japanese flags fluttered in the same breeze
that carried clouds of black smoke
and cries of agony.
Shops and factories and houses destroyed.
Nothing left but piles of ashes
and old women, wailing,
sifting through them
to find anything they once owned.

So many terrible sounds.
So many terrible wounds.
Women and young girls dragged
from homes or refugee camps
used and abused in unspeakable ways
and tossed away.
Apart from the missionaries,
Iris was the only foreigner left.
All the other reporters had gone
or been expelled.

Being foreign gave her some protection
not offered to those terrified Chinese girls,
but she was far from safe.

This is what she owned:
40 Chinese dollars
1 pair of trousers
1 shirt
1 change of underwear.
And me.

The city reeked of death and decay.

Iris had made a will, years ago, in Auckland.
She included the typewriter,
but not me.

Perhaps she couldn't imagine life
without me,
or perhaps she thought
I had no worth to anyone else.

But now,
in case the worst happened,
she wrote letters home,
thinking they might be her last.

I can't imagine what her family thought,
when those letters
finally arrived.

Dear Old Mother, Dad, Hazel, Edna and Ruth – and Dan'l the pup,

I have to write to you jointly because one letter each is just now impossible …

The Chinese city of Hsuchowfu, where I've been staying both before and after visiting the Chinese eastern front north of Pihsien, fell into Japanese hands this morning, and thousands of them – tanks, cavalry, infantry – have been trooping through the little cobbled streets while bombers simply rained down bombs on the only exit roads …

I don't know quite how I stand, as the one and only British subject in the city, a writer, and a woman writer at that. So Hsuchowfu is either an adventure or the adventure! …

My work was the only thing I could do besides caring for people, and I want that to live, if anything of me lives.

So long now, my darlings, and don't forget 92 Northland Rd and long ago 9 Blythe St, Berhampore, were always addresses in which I took great pride. A family is a story, and I'm just one chapter in it, hurriedly and badly written. But I hope the story goes on and on, and is happy if possible, but strong if happiness isn't possible yet.

Your own
Iris

No one knew where we were.
This was when Iris started to make headlines around the world.

NEW ZEALAND JOURNALIST MISSING.
JAPANESE SEARCHING FOR MISS IRIS WILKINSON.
SHANGHAI, MAY 27.
The Japanese authorities are searching for the New Zealand journalist, Miss Iris Wilkinson, who departed on a donkey from Hsuchow to the northeastern front, which is now overrun by Japanese troops retreating from Langfeng. She may possibly have taken refuge with the missionaries, who are determined to remain at Hsuchow to safeguard Chinese refugees.

STOP PRESS. MISSING WOMAN JOURNALIST.
Miss Iris Wilkinson, who is reported missing in China, is better known as Robin Hyde. She left New Zealand in January with the intention of proceeding via Shanghai, Kobe, Vladivostok, and the Trans-Siberia Railway to Russia and thence to England, but her itinerary was interrupted by the lengthening of her sojourn in China, where she engaged in journalistic work. Her family last heard from her from Canton on April 2. She intended to go to Hankow and then as far as she could towards the war zone, writing for various periodicals, but this was to occupy only a month. —*Evening Star*, 28 May 1938

Better known as Robin Hyde

Before Derek, there was Robin.

You know about Derek,
but you don't know about Robin.

It all goes back to
Rotorua,
or perhaps even further back, to
the war.

Nellie's darling brother Bertie,
killed at Gallipoli,
left some money to the family.
Iris decided to use her share
for a trip to Rotorua
where the hot mineral baths
might help her stiff leg.

She was 19 years old.
In Rotorua, her life would change again.

Apart from South Africa, which she couldn't remember,
one childhood trip to Australia,
which she could barely remember,
some family holidays across the harbour in Days Bay
and Easter with Harry in Auckland,
Iris had seen little except Wellington.
Rotorua was a strange new world
and she loved it all –
the bubbling hot pools,
shooting geysers, the steaming lake,
mud cauldrons that leaped and lurched,
Māori kids diving for tourists' pennies.
The dazzling sunsets.

Rotorua was
sulphur-smelling baths
that turned white skin lobster-scarlet.

Rotorua was
warm and buoyant baths
as calm as meditation
and fizzy radium baths
frothing with bubbles like champagne.

And Rotorua was
Frederick de Mulford Hyde:
aged 27, war veteran, air force pilot,
tall, thin, dashing, elegant, well dressed,
apparently rich.

Iris felt almost well again.
Nerves, the doctors said. That was the problem.

But they recommended another operation
and after that, her knee was much worse.

On her 20th birthday,
she went to say goodbye to Frederick,
thought he blanched at the sight of her crutches,
asked him about certain 'symptoms'.
'No,' he declared. 'Impossible.'

But it was possible.
It was more than possible.
In April, a doctor confirmed it.
'You're right up against it, then?' he said,
not unkindly, just stating the facts:
young
single
disabled
pregnant.

Iris has always been good at keeping secrets
but Nellie guessed something was up
and got the truth out of her.
Iris told nobody else
except Gwen, her oldest friend.
Her sisters didn't know.
Her father didn't know.

Frederick said they could marry
but Iris said she would have the baby first,
and if she didn't die in childbirth
she would think about marriage then.
I don't think she was joking.

Having a baby was dangerous. Death in childbirth
was still a real threat, not a joke.

She told people she was going to Sydney for
specialist knee treatment.
It sounded necessary and important:
specialist knee treatment.

I'm the one who hears all the conversations,
even those Iris has with herself.
I'm the one who's there when she can't sleep.

Only Nellie and Gwen and Frederick and I knew the truth
about why Iris was sailing on the *Awatea*.
Only Nellie and Gwen and Frederick and I
and the tiny bud growing inside her.

It was exciting to be boarding an ocean liner.
I didn't know, then, about the many voyages
we would go on together, how I would be carried
on rattly buses and trucks,
thrown in after her through the
open windows of a Chinese train.
I didn't know, then, about the many wharves
we would leave from, or arrive at,
most often with no one to greet or farewell us,
not like this:
the band playing,
the streamers, the bouquets,
the last hugs, the tears and waving hands.
Nellie and the sisters.
Gwen, pushing through the crowds,
thrusting a small parcel into Iris's hands.

In the cabin
Iris unwrapped the parcel.
Inside, beneath a layer of tissue,
was a pair of tiny blue baby shoes
embroidered with cherry blossom.

She cried and cried and cried.

Thorny mandarins and poetry

Three days later, the *Awatea* sailed up Sydney Harbour.
Iris gripped me tightly
and I stood as straight and tall as I could,
knowing she had no one but me to help her.

She found a place to live, in Redfern,
because she liked the name of the suburb.
Typical Iris, fixated on words.
She boarded with a family:
Letty, husband Art, one-legged grandad,
four-year-old Molly, a rosella parrot,
two dogs and a horse called Abe.
She used a fake wedding ring
and a fake name with *Mrs* in it.
Letty wasn't fooled
though she was happy to use Iris as extra help
in return for turning a blind eye.
Iris was pregnant and paying for her room
but she ended up sweeping, dusting,
making beds, emptying out slops.

Frederick sent money for board and some extra
but there wasn't a lot to spare.

Iris lived on thorny mandarins,
much sweeter than their name,
small and juicy and bright green,
you could get thirty for sixpence at the market.
We visited a department store
as grand as a palace, and wandered the bustling floors
looking at things she couldn't afford
but Iris bought some anyway
for the baby, who was getting bigger
every day.

We visited the Sydney public library,
took refuge in rows of books
and poetry.

Then there was an argument,
some sudden flare-up,
and Letty wanted her out, there and then,
so within an hour Iris was packed and out the door
and we went traipsing round for rooms again.

This time we were lucky.
Iris found a better place to live
and made a good friend,
Kay, a nurse.

Back then, Iris and I were still getting used to each other.
Me, to the feel of her hand.
Her, to my heft and weight.
Already I had a sense of her energy and impatience
and that she was not always
the easiest person to be friends with,
but with Kay, she was happy and at ease.

Iris read an article about babies being mixed up
in nursing homes and Kay laughed at her.
'That won't happen, Iris,' she assured her,
but Iris went and bought a bangle anyway
to put on the baby's wrist,
so it couldn't, definitely wouldn't ever happen.

Then it was time for the baby to arrive.

A bangle and a name

The hospital was cool and clean,
shady verandahs engulfed in purple jacaranda blossom.
At night, the lights of the city
sparkled in the distance.
It felt like a safe place
to welcome her baby into the world.

It took hours and hours,
a day and a night.
I wasn't needed, tossed aside.
But I could hear everything:
the screams, the curt instructions.

When it was all over
I heard the nurse.
'No, it's not all right, Mrs …
the poor little chap.'

His small face.
His tiny feet.
They let her see him

and touch his soft cheek,
still warm,
but not hold him.
She made them put on the bangle she'd bought,
even though there was no chance, now,
that he would get mixed up with another baby.
That was all she could give him,
his nine months growing,
the bangle,
and his name.
Names are important.
She named him
Christopher Robin Hyde.

White clouds, mourning

Birds screeched like witches
and bats flapped through the dark.
The moon overhead was cloaked
in white clouds, mourning
for her little dead son.

Later, we buried him in a cemetery.
He seemed such a tiny mite
to be left in this vast place
all by himself.
Only the beds of white daisies
gave her any comfort.
At night, I heard her weeping
for her lost child.

Later, Iris forgot the name of the cemetery.
All she knew was that there were daisies
and so many headstones.

Ferries criss-crossed the harbour.
The sea was just as blue
the grass just as lurid green
the sun just as warm
the skyscrapers just as tall

but the sun couldn't warm her
and the skyscrapers hemmed her in.
People hurried past on the streets,
smiled and chatted in cafés.

In all of that vast city
so few people knew
her son was dead.

When we sailed back to Auckland,
Iris left the new baby clothes behind,
but she kept Gwen's tiny blue baby shoes
embroidered with cherry blossom.

What she didn't expect to find:
Frederick, newly married
to a woman eight years older than him,
the woman who owned the house
where Iris and Frederick used to meet.

Now her life started to change
again.

She couldn't sleep.
Bought sleeping pills from a chemist,
then more
from another chemist.
More, from another.
Another hospital.
Another doctor.

'You've been romancing, young woman,'
he said brusquely. 'Well, where's the baby?'

'My son is dead,' she said.
My son is dead.
My son is dead.
My son is dead.

That is the story of Robin.

Insomnia

This is how it goes.
Not for me.
I don't need sleep.
But for Iris.

Can't sleep
Can't sleep
Can't sleep

Worry
Worry
Pills

Nightmares
Broken
        sleep
Muttered
        cries

Can't sleep
Can't sleep
Can't sleep

Worry

Pills

Names

Iris had many names.
As children's editor for the *Farmers' Advocate*
(on the page opposite 'Women's Sphere'.
Newspaper owners had clear views
about what women wanted to read
and where was their sphere),
she answered letters as Mary Advocate.

What a pity your pony is lame, John. Is he any better?
Life on the sheep farm must be very interesting, Catherine.
You certainly had an adventure with your pony, Trixie!
Do you help in milking all those cows, Kathleen?

But sometimes, Mary Advocate
shook her imagination loose.

I have a sore throat that makes me feel as if I were something between a giraffe and a boa constrictor and had been fed on prickly pears and hedgehogs for a month.
You must live in a very interesting place, Laura,
among all that dark owl-haunted bush.

Don't you wish that for one moment we could sit on
the magic carpet of the Arabian Nights *and go*
sailing through the blue sky with the world at our feet?

As parliamentary reporter for the *Dominion*
(but in a light-hearted way,
the sort of thing women would like to read,
not too serious, they told her),
she took her place in the ladies gallery
to watch the men at work, for her column
'Peeps at Parliament' by Novitia.

On the *Wanganui Chronicle*, she wrote as Margot.

'Mrs Challis' was another name.

Why am I telling you about all her names?
Because, a few months after Sydney,
she was sent to Queen Mary Hospital,
Hanmer Springs, for five months of rest,
hot mineral baths, physio, massage
and long forest walks.

Hanmer didn't feel like a hospital.
There was tennis and golf
and a tea kiosk for scones and tea,
but this was where shell-shocked soldiers
recovered, as best they could, from the horrors
of the Great War. Where they tried to wipe
hideous sights from their memories,
or at least learn to live with them.

Hanmer was
coloured autumn leaves
the smell of pine and cold
bare naked trees
flakes of early snow like drifting specks of light
snow falling with a soft thump off
weighted branches
frozen puddles that crunched underfoot
the guardian snow-topped mountains
the circling hills
the rosy sunset light
the silver moonlight.

Hanmer was
where the words came back
and Iris started to write again.

Hanmer was
where she took up her new pen name.
Her little son was gone from the world,
but he would live on in the name
she chose to write under.
Miss Iris Wilkinson,
better known as the author Robin Hyde.

On and on

In Hsuchow, a few shops reopened:
barbers, teashops, but there was not much food.
There was no way out except on foot,
which was surely impossible,
so that's what Iris decided we would do.

On 30 May, with a mug around her neck
and a case full of papers
– not even her blanket, this time –
we set off along the railway line to Chengchow.

It was brave and adventurous
and slightly mad.

China is a vast country,
hundreds of thousands of *li*
from north to south and west to east,
which I knew because we trundled across it by train
for hours, for whole days, sometimes.
Trying to walk across it, even a part of it,
was crazy. But that's what Iris decided.
That's what she did.

It was brave and adventurous
and slightly mad,
but that was Iris.

We had no map, just a scrap of paper
with the names of railway stations
written in Chinese characters,
so we kept to the railway tracks,
our only clue to direction.

Every few *li* there was a railway station
manned by Japanese soldiers.
At the first station, they were friendly
and gave her food and hot sweet tea,
but we didn't stay.

We plodded on.

On and on, plod, plod, plod.
Getting late. Getting dark.
Where would we sleep?
Under a hedge? An abandoned barn?
A ruined village? The next station?

Then, in a few confused minutes, everything changed.
A steep bit of track, a peasant going past,
a light in the distance, some small train or trolley
approaching. He got a fright and pushed Iris.
Did he mean to be kind? *Out of the way,*
look out, was he warning her?
Iris fell, with a cry of dismay, tumbling down the bank,
and I fell after her. The bank was covered with bushes
sprouting thorns as sharp as needles
and one scratched me down my whole length.
Night settled over us. Iris lay huddled and still,
then at last she stirred,
but I could tell from how she pressed her hand
against her eye that it was painful.
As daylight arrived, she groped around for me,
slowly pulled us back up to the track.
A bit groggy
but at least she could still walk
and see out of one eye.

At the next railway station,
they made her lie down,
put a cold cloth on her eyes,
insisted she stay the night on a stretcher.

A Japanese doctor from a troop train
put drops in her eyes.
In the morning
we walked on.

Iris looked thin –
gaunt, even –
exhausted
pale
half starved
dirty and unkempt.

One eye black and swollen
clothes ragged and holey
shoes falling to bits.
If she collapsed here –
she mustn't –
nobody might ever know
what happened to her.

Now she had started, she must keep going.

Don't give up, I told her at each step.
Don't give up.
Don't give up.

Don't look, I told her sometimes,
but she always looked. She was a writer.

Dead bodies
lay strewn under the tracks,
unburied, some chewed by dogs.
Their clothes torn and bloody,
flesh turning an odd colour,

streams of ants and beetles
scurrying into their nostrils and open throats.

Some boys gave us a ride in a wheelbarrow
for five dollars.
Peasants digging in the fields
turned their stolid gaze on us
as if surprise was an emotion they had no room for
and nothing could astonish them again
now they had lived through this war.

Don't give up

Don't give up, I told her.
Don't give up.
Don't give up.

Remember our trip to Queenstown,
I told her. *Don't give up.*

In Queenstown, Iris had decided to climb Ben Lomond,
5000 feet high, almost a proper mountain.
I wanted to tell her it was a bad idea,
but I knew she wouldn't listen.
She didn't listen to the people at the boarding house.
You need a 2 am start. It's not for women.
Women who do it have to spend a week in bed afterwards.
Sunday was gloriously fine.
A chap called Gordon, staying at the same hotel,
was keen for a walk, too. We set out in the afternoon …
a bit late, as it turned out.

Tussock, birch forest, mountain daisies,
the first patches of snow,
a hut where Iris hoped for tea and a billy
but found none.

It was a long steady uphill trek.
I wanted Iris to turn around.
I wanted her to remember that this was only up
and she still had to come down
but she was determined to get to the top.
She was always so determined.

It was ridiculous
for someone with a stiff leg
to attempt to climb Ben Lomond.

It was brave and adventurous
and slightly mad,
but that was Iris.

After a while, Gordon hinted the same,
but she wouldn't listen.

We reached the top.
Sunset coloured the summit
like a flamboyant painting, but the descent
was as bad as I feared. Getting dark,
no food, stumbling down a barely visible track.

I did my best
but the slippery shale and stones
slid underfoot like marbles.
Iris was exhausted. I could tell
from her tight grip.

Don't give up, I told her.
Don't give up.
Don't give up.

At times she lay down in the tussock
to escape the icy biting wind.
Finally, after midnight,
she and Gordon stumbled into the hotel,
too bone-weary to feel any triumph.

Don't give up, I told her now.
Don't give up.
Don't give up.

But I should have known
she wouldn't ever give up.
The same determination that keeps her bashing at her
typewriter, meeting deadlines, staring down rejections,
powers her writing, powers her up mountains,
kept her plodding along the train tracks,
refusing to admit defeat.

If you were Chinese,
we would shoot you

At the next station there were many soldiers.
Iris showed them her pass.
She told them she was a reporter.
They thought she was a spy.
If you were Chinese, we would shoot you, they yelled,
and said she couldn't walk on the railway tracks.

They took us to the other side of a village
and left us there. Iris waited until they had gone,
and then we made our way back to the tracks.
We didn't know where else to go.
It was the only way we had.

The next villagers were kind.
They gave us loaves of fresh bread
but wouldn't let us stay overnight.
We were a danger to them.
If the Japanese came and found us there,
anything could happen, to us or to them,
so they sent us on our way, and we plodded on.

We slept in a field
under the thin shelter of bushes.
Drizzly rain spattered over us.

The next morning
it was daylight when Iris awoke,
and when she stood up
and brushed herself down,
a group of peasants working in the field
approached us, staring, talking
excitedly amongst themselves,
incomprehensible to us.

They came closer. Surrounded us.
Calmly they took everything from her.
Hands reached out for
her mug
her case of papers

her money
her brown silk hat
her green coat
her sunglasses
her rings
and me.

They carried us away.
Behind us she sank to the ground, sobbing.

Voices rose and fell above my head.

I did not know what would happen next,
and as we jogged over the fields and the distance
between us stretched
I felt that I would break or snap or shatter.

Urgent voices above me.
Then, just as incomprehensibly,
they carried us back and returned everything:
mug
case
money
hat
coat
sunglasses
rings
and me.

What did they think?
Did they think she was Japanese?
Did they find the stamp in her passport?
It was impossible to tell.

A band of Japanese soldiers appeared.
The peasants scattered,
melting away into the fields
like stones camouflaged in the tall grass.
The soldiers insisted Iris got on their train
going back towards Hsuchow
where we had just come from.
No, no, they told her, *the train is going
all the way through to Tsingtao
and you can get a boat from there to Hong Kong.*
But when they made us get off the train
we were back in Hsuchow.

All
that
walking
for
nothing.

MISSING JOURNALIST. BROADCAST FROM CHINA. WATCHING FIGHT FROM HILL. [BY TELEGRAPH – PRESS ASSOCIATION] WELLINGTON, TUESDAY. Several Chinese residents in Wellington about May 19 heard a message broadcast from Station 2ZK, Hong Kong, which stated that a New Zealand woman had been watching at Suchow a battle from the top of a nearby hill. As her position appeared to be very dangerous, the Chinese were much concerned. The Chinese Consulate has been informed by the listeners, as the incident may be a clue to the whereabouts of Miss Iris Wilkinson (Robin Hyde),

who was reported in a cablegram received on Saturday
to be missing in the Suchow area.
—*New Zealand Herald*, 1 June 1938

Some, but not all

Back in Hsuchow, Iris told Dr Nettie
she was going to try again.
This time in the other direction,
from the North Station
to Tsingtao, 300 miles away.

She got another pass:
permission to travel to Tsingtao,
but the officials at North Station shook their heads.
No foreigners on troop trains, they said,
so Iris set off to walk along the tracks
hoping to find an official at another smaller station
who would let her on board.

A sentry hauled her into a shed
fumbled around with her clothes
but he found her pass instead,
and it was official enough to impress him
so he let us continue.

Some of the Japanese soldiers were kind.
They let her climb onto the back of a troop train,
but the next station master made her get down again.

Some of the Japanese soldiers were kind,
but not all. These soldiers
ignored her pass and passport

and marched her back to the station.
One grabbed her by the arms,
but she managed to swipe him
across the legs with – me!
The first time I'd ever hit anyone like that.
It was a shock to me, and him.
Maybe also to Iris. He swore and let her go
and looked at her with more respect.

Some of the Japanese soldiers were kind
but not these ones.
They twisted her arms behind her back.
One man barked questions at her,
shouted in her face, 'Spy! Spy!'

Of course she was not a spy.
Anyone could see that.

They kicked me aside.

Slap! Crack!
The man slapped her across the face.
The impact jarred right through me.

Again,
Slap!
Again,
Slap!

Iris's eyes blazed.
She hadn't come this far
to give in to a bully.

Slap!

Slap!
I gave up counting.
Couldn't he see how thin and weak
and sick she was?
Couldn't he see her poor, sore, bloodshot eyes?

Couldn't he see
that she was a threat
to nobody?

Couldn't he just
let her go
on her way?

They started to rip off her clothes
looking for papers to prove her spy identity.
What saved her:
she had a bag around her neck
with her money in
and she threw the coins in their faces
out of bravery
or despair
or panic
or no other options.
Everyone froze
and I thought: is this the end?

But it was a brilliant strategy
that even a real spy might have applauded

because they thought that
she thought
they were mere thieves and robbers,

so they were embarrassed and ashamed
of how they'd treated her
when she was no spy, no one important,
just another fleeing refugee.

Some of the Japanese soldiers were kind.
They gave her back her papers and money,
brought rice and stewed apricots to eat
and straw to lie on.

And the next morning
we kept walking
through deserted burnt-out villages
through the rain
through the dark.
We slept in the blackened shell of a building.

And the next morning
we kept walking.

Some of the Japanese soldiers were kind.
These ones asked lots of questions
gave her tinned peaches to eat
and a bed to lie on,
finally put her on a troop train,
at Lincheng, with a soldier as bodyguard.

And at last, we reached
the sea, at Tsingtao.

NEW ZEALAND AUTHORESS. MISS WILKINSON
AT SHANGHAI. RECEIVED JULY 6, 9.30 AM
SHANGHAI, JULY 5. Feeling tired, but well, the

New Zealander, Miss Iris Wilkinson (Robin Hyde, the authoress) has arrived from Tsingtao, which she reached partly afoot and partly by a Japanese troop train. Miss Wilkinson was recently reported to be missing in the vicinity of Tsingtao, and fears were entertained for her safety. However, she was later reported to have reached Tsingtao.
—*Manawatu Standard*, 6 July 1938

MISS WILKINSON. RECOVERY IN HOSPITAL.
RECEIVED JULY 16, 9.45 AM HONG KONG, JULY 15.
The New Zealander, Miss Iris Wilkinson ('Robin Hyde'), who was missing recently in China, is recovering slowly in hospital. Fears for the safety of Miss Wilkinson were caused when no report was received of her whereabouts for some time. Finally she arrived at Tsingtao in an exhausted condition.
—*Manawatu Standard*, 16 July 1938

Seasons

Tsingtao is where I started my story,
if you remember. But we didn't stay long.

We set sail south again, via Shanghai.
On 11 July, we arrived back in Hong Kong
on the *Tjinegara*.

It was the rainy season
in Hong Kong.

The season of mist
swirling round the hills.

The season of steaming rain
slashing on windowpanes
beating on umbrellas
rushing down streets
and steep crowded lanes.

The season of thunderstorms
like bombs exploding.
The season of lightning
like fires igniting.

It was the season of sickness.
We were sick of travel
sick of moving on
sick of war
and suffering
sick of being foreign.

Heartsick
and actually sick.

Or Iris was.

It was the sad season.
The homesick season.

A cheap hotel, and then we ended up
in hospital
again.

Moonlight shone through hospital glass.
White coats, squeaky hospital trolleys.
Doctors, nurses, poking, prodding,
measuring, testing.

Iris lay in hospital under clean white sheets,
remembering those 22 Chinese soldiers,
their filthy bandages, their brave eyes.
It was quiet here, no guns.
Just the hiss of the rain.

In China the war raged on.
Her heart was still there.

So tired

A reporter came to interview Iris,
but she was so tired that
she had to rest against the pillows
between sentences.

I've walked a long way with her,
many miles, hundreds of *li*
but I never get tired.
I wonder how it feels.

I lay in a corner of the room
and let her words wash over me.

… *I can only talk of it in scraps*
… *I heard the guns muttering*
… *bombs dropped*
… *I can hardly bear to talk of it*
… *hundreds of people killed*
… *trapped in the ruins*
… *women and children*
… *I can only talk of it in scraps*
… *the screams and moans of those unhappy victims*

The reporter nodded as she scribbled away,
but she didn't see what we saw.

I thought about all the faces.
People we didn't know,
who were mothers, fathers, aunts,
uncles, grandparents,
sisters, brothers, cousins.
My memory unspooled …
hurrying feet, urgent voices,
frightened eyes,
loaded wheelbarrows, backs
bowed under burdens
(sacks of rice, bundles of clothes,
sleeping babies).
A mother's hand clutching a child's.

… I can only talk of it in scraps

Not the first time

This was not Iris's first time in hospital,
far from it.

There was the time when her knee was first treated,
when lions roared at night through the Newtown streets.
I've told you about that.

There was the time when Robin was born.
And died. I've told you about that.

There was the time in Hanmer Springs.
I've told you about that.

There was the time when Derek was born.
I've told you about that.

But there was also the time in Auckland.
I haven't told you about that.

In 1931, Iris got a job on the *Observer*.
(Derek was a baby, still in Palmerston North.)
The *Observer* came out every Thursday
and the work was relentless, week after week
after week. The deadline couldn't be missed.
It was a frantic life, out all the time,
chasing stories, then tapping away at her typewriter
late at night, writing them up.

One of her first jobs:
we were at Devonport Navy yards on 3 February
to report on the departure of HMS *Dunedin*
for England, just as news spread
of a huge earthquake in Hawke's Bay,
where fires were burning, people trapped
under collapsed buildings.
The ship was ordered to Napier instead
with doctors, nurses and medical stores.

A hard time to be a woman

It was the middle of the Depression.
Soup kitchens.
Vagrant women.
Riots in Queen Street.
Thousands out of work.

Random strangers climbed the stairs
to the *Observer* office,
people peddling religion,
faith healers promising cures for everything.
All those returned soldiers down on their luck,
eking out a poor living by selling boot laces.

Iris was always on the side of the underdog,
always fighting what wasn't fair.
It was the Depression. All workers
had to pay an unemployment tax:
one shilling in the pound.
Women had to pay it,
but if they lost their jobs
they didn't get the unemployment benefit.

That wasn't fair.

It was a hard time to be a woman,
trying to earn her way in the world
with no help.
Especially a woman writer.
Especially an unmarried mother
with a secret child.

So many secrets

1932: Derry was 15 months old,
toddling and gorgeous. Iris sent money
for Mrs Rattan to bring him up on the train
and for a few delirious weeks
she and her friend Beula

looked after him at the Burwood.
They fed him on grapes and tomatoes
but that couldn't last –
a baby at the Burwood,
or the tomatoes-and-grapes diet –
and Beula had to return to Christchurch,
so they went hunting for a foster home
and they found the Hutsons, Ben and Alice.

Iris was always good at keeping secrets.
Her workmates didn't know about Derek.
Her sisters didn't know.
Nellie still didn't know.
Derry, that toddling sweetheart,
was her secret.

Her father didn't know about Derek
and he never would,
or if he did, that was his secret
and he never said.

So many secrets.

Out of work

Thursday 25 May 1933:
we didn't know it then,
but her last piece appeared in the *Observer*.

A few days later, they called Iris into the office.
Her job was gone.

It was a disaster
for her and for Derek.

She didn't get the unemployment benefit
because of being a woman,
but women needed money to live on, too,
to pay rent and buy food and a few degrees of warmth,
and she needed to pay the Hutsons
for looking after Derek.
Derek's father was supposed to send money,
a few shillings a week, but that didn't always happen.

And it was the middle of the Depression.
Thousands already out of work.
No jobs.

A quiet splash

The next day, we went walking down Queen Street.
Iris was distracted, at times distraught.
We ducked in and out of back streets,
side streets and alleyways
on haphazard routes, but all the time – I realised,
as the gulls shrieked above us –
getting closer to the harbour.
We crossed the last road.
Two boys were larking about on the wharf.
Iris waited for them to leave
and then I knew what she was planning to do.

Iris,
no.

She kept going,
laid me down,
waited hardly a second then,
with no fuss,
jumped

and I couldn't do anything.

A quiet splash.
Then gasping, thrashing about,
feet running, yells and shouts.
They were hauling her up, water dripping off her.

Someone tripped over me, picked me up (thank goodness).
She shouted, flailed at her rescuers.
They bundled us into a vehicle,
while onlookers gawked, open-mouthed.
Next thing, we were in the cells under the hospital.
They brought her towels, brandy, a steaming hot drink;
dressed her in a billowing white hospital gown.
Her teeth were chattering, from cold, or shock, or both.
I would shiver, too, if I could.

Whatever she meant to do, she didn't do it,
and now the police were here, because suicide
was not illegal (obviously, if you managed it,
you were beyond the reach of the law), but
attempting to commit suicide was.
You could be arrested and charged,
for being miserable, for being at the end
of your tether, for seeing too many problems
and no solutions, and that's what happened.
You have to appear in court, they told her.

The Auckland Magistrates Court.
She pleaded not guilty, an 'accidental fall'.
Case adjourned to 4 December.
Name suppressed.
Another secret to keep.

But the questions hadn't gone away.
How to earn a living?
How to pay for Derek's care?

Her guardian angels

Then two guardian doctor-angels came into her life.
Dr Henry Buchanan, medical superintendent
at Auckland Mental Hospital, Avondale.
Dr Gilbert Tothill, psychiatrist.

Dr Buchanan suggested she move into the hospital
as a boarder, a voluntary patient.
She could stay in the Grey Lodge.
It was our home for the next three months.

Iris went home for a quick visit.
Her sisters didn't know about the wharf
or her temporary home in the hospital.
Her father didn't know.
Only Nellie knew.
Secrets, again.

On 4 December: back before the court.
Case discharged.

The next day, we went walking down Queen Street.
Iris was distracted, at times distraught.
Not the wharf this time,
just the middle of a busy street.
The world was too much.
It was all too much.
Iris fell to pieces again.

Back to Avondale,
back to the Grey Lodge
Our home for the next three years.

The Grey Lodge

The Lodge had stained-glass windows
staircases with polished banisters
beds in dormitories
beds on the closed-in verandah

but Iris was given a bedroom to herself
and an attic, where she could bash away
on her typewriter.

The children out on the street
pointed and giggled, called it names:
the loony bin, the madhouse,
dared each other to enter the gates.
'You'll catch it!'
'You'll go crazy!'
Then ran away shrieking
in fear and delight.

Iris was a model patient,
given leave to go into the city
several times a week
as long as she was back by 8 PM.

She saw Derry when she could,
bought him coats and clothing when she could.
For his fourth Christmas, she made him a
book of rhymes, *by his own Mother*
who hopes to have them printed
with funny pictures,
one fine day.
But it was the Depression,
and the Hutsons left in search of work,
found it at a railway camp at Nūhaka.
Apparently he was happy,
but it was so very far away.

It was always noisy at the Lodge:
radios blaring
people yelling
doors banging
brooms mops and pails
arguments squabbles sudden fights wild accusations
fourpence taken from someone's locker
patients prowling the corridors for hours
shouts and sobs and sharp-tongued nurses.

Sometimes she could hardly bear it,
but it was our sanctuary.

And Iris started to write again.

Now you know

Now you know about Iris and me.
You know who Derek is.
You know who Robin was.
You know who Harry was.
You know who I am.

You know nearly everything now, all the secrets
locked inside her and me.
You know about family and friends and lovers
and children and war and words released
like burning flames.

Getting better

In Hong Kong, Iris came out of hospital.
We took a rickshaw ride to The Peak
its steep slopes a glorious mass of wild verbenas and lilies
and the air fluttering with butterflies,
black and jade, grey and turquoise.

Iris still had her Trans-Siberian rail ticket
but there were more visa problems
because of the war, and finally, regretfully, she gave up
on the Trans-Siberian dream, cashed in her ticket.

On 11 August, we left Hong Kong on the *Serooskerk*
to Manila and Singapore,
where they put her in hospital at the Navy base
to wait for a bigger ship with a doctor on board.
In Singapore, she bought Derek
a small stuffed crocodile.
What eight-year-old boy wouldn't like that?

On 26 August, we sailed on the
Johan van Oldenbarnevelt
via Belawan, Sabang, Colombo, Suez, Port Said,
Genoa, Villefranche, Algiers
to Southampton, then the train up to London.
Iris was in England at last, the faraway home
that her mother Nellie longed to see
but never reached.

Safety pins

What happened next?
Did we see English bluebells
under English woods
in an English spring,
owls and foxgloves,
English heather
on English hills?

Things haven't worked out quite as we planned.
As Iris once said,
'Chance is the lovely lord of any journey.'
But this time, chance
has not been kind to her.

In London, we met some familiar faces.
Her friend Beula, who had helped feed Derek
on tomatoes and grapes.
James Bertram, who had taken her to Macao.
Charles Brasch, New Zealand writer and scholar.
James and Charles were younger, wealthier, more
confident than Iris. Life seemed easier to them.
Was it being men? Or having money?
Or both?

The bluebells and primroses were a thrill
as were the magic street names of London:
Piccadilly, Trafalgar Square, Oxford Street, Soho,
and its churches, palaces and cathedrals:
St Paul's, Buckingham Palace, Westminster Abbey.
But London is also a city of grimy old buildings,
noise and clatter and traffic.
Even with my help, Iris couldn't manage
the stairs on the Underground.
We took the red buses instead.

England didn't feel like home.
Chestnut trees and weeping willows
made me think of Christchurch.
Birch trees and berries,
sharp frosts and leaves turning crimson

then golden daffodils in the spring
reminded me of Hanmer.

The green dappled forests
were nothing like kauri forests,
trees like cathedrals,
the towering majesty of Tāne Mahuta.

The children in gloves and hats and warm boots,
sailing boats on the Round Pond
in Kensington Gardens,
reminded Iris of Derek.
The chubby rosy-cheeked Renoir children
in the National Gallery
reminded her of Derek.
But he was so far away.

This was her life in England:
No money.
Sick.
Poor.
A caravan with no toilet.
Winter clothes from a local charity
held together with safety pins.
Rain. Sleet. Snow.
Books not selling well, the publishers told her,
but still
writing
writing
writing.

No real days, only brief candles of pale light
between the white morning fog and the evening one,

deep yellow, settling already at three o'clock,
with the bare trees of the woods
sticking up as if they were drowned.

A cold Christmas,
a week in Middlesex Hospital,
with the Hermes and me and all her manuscripts,
where they fed her red wet blobs on a plate,
raw liver, to fight anaemia.
Then the Hospital for Tropical Diseases,
which sounds exotic
if you're not in it.

Some nasty disease

Turns out
Iris has
picked up
in China
some nasty
disease called
sprue.

Runny poos,
that kind
of thing.
She needs
to be
in hospital
again,
not in
a caravan

with no
toilet.

I don't get sick
with my hard wooden body,
my one strong limb,
my one good foot.

A little worn, a little damaged,
but still working as I'm meant to.
This scratch
from the same thorns that poked into Iris's eye.
Another scratch
from jumping out of a truck in an air raid.
A black boot mark from a kick.
Untold scuff marks
from being tossed into corners.
That red mark
could be a smear of blood
but I'm not sure whose,
or where it came from.

Homeless

Homeless again,
we moved from place to place.
Caravan, hotel, boarding house,
staying with friends
and some new-found cousins.

Homeless.
This is how it was back in New Zealand when

Dr Tothill left the Grey Lodge for a new job.
He had been her sounding board there, her anchor.
He'd encouraged Iris to write,
helped her unleash a torrent of words
but with him gone, she was adrift
and restless.

After the Grey Lodge, *homeless*, we moved from place
to place: a lodge here, a rented cottage there,
a friend's bach in their garden.
A month at Whangaroa,
a harbour dark as greenstone
where the *Boyd* burned in 1809
and the old folk still hobbled on walking sticks –
my remote cousins –
made out of wood from the ship.
At Whangaroa, our cabin was wobbly and draughty
with sliding wooden panels for windows,
a lamp for a light and no bath,
but sunsets like a flight of flamingos
and starry nights like concert halls for
singing Māori voices and guitars.

Iris did some more work for the *Observer.*
We went to teacup readings and palm readings,
faith-healing sessions, prisons and cocktail parties,
Chinese pakapoo dens, Turkish baths,
dances and race meetings,
glittering soirées at Government House
and the Hospital Relief Depot for the unemployed.

Iris would venture anywhere
in search of copy. With me in one hand,
grasping the gangway rope in the other,
she went out to gather stories
from visiting ships.

She chatted to lads queuing up overnight
to nab tickets for the Springboks test.
She talked to nurses heading to the Spanish Civil War.
She took Māori language lessons, caught the bus
to Ōrākei and scrambled up path and hillside
to houses, tents, church cemetery and meeting house
to talk to the people clinging onto their papakāinga.
Their heart is with their land, she wrote.

Back then, she wasn't sleeping well.
She had nightmares, as she often did.
She had plans and dreams,
one big dream: go to England,
publish a book that will really take off,
make money, make her name, come back
so she and Derek could be together
at last.

That's how we ended up here,
homeless.

Missing home.
Missing China.
Iris wanted to go back
(to home? to China?)
but there was no money for either.

In London, murmuring voices
in St Dunstan's Chapel prayed for peace
because now war loomed here too
like a ship towering above us at the wharf,
and nobody cared much about a war
in some remote country
where people are different
and the placenames hard to pronounce.

She is sick
Poor
Homesick
Heartsick
But she just keeps on
Writing
Writing
Writing.
This is how I will always remember her.

At Bishop's Barn

It's April 1939,
a spring morning,
and we are outside a farmhouse
deep in the English countryside.

Iris sits on the rough grass
in the shade of a tree,
her legs, cradled by a low table,
stick out in front of her.
The table holds her notes and
her Hermes Baby portable typewriter

that she has been reunited with.
We are a good team, the three of us,
Iris, me and the Hermes.

You can't see me.
I'm sprawled in the grass
out of sight, but I'm here,
in the background,
because I always am.
Iris isn't thinking about me.
She doesn't need me right now.
She is busy,
working,
writing.
This is how I like to think of her:
Iris at her most Iris,
words clattering out of her,
pages spilling out of the Hermes
onto the grass.
The few days at Bishop's Barn
staying with her friend Charles Brasch
are a restful interlude.
It's not typical of our life
since we reached England.

In a vast and mysterious country
far away, across many seas,
war is still raging.

A few months ago
we were in that country. China.

Now we are far away
and all Iris can do is write about it
as she promised she would,
fingers clattering on the typewriter keys,
and hope that people will read,
because that's what she does.

Her fingers typing
sometimes hesitant
as soft showers in an English spring,
sometimes urgent and violent
as monsoon rain
drumming on a roof in Hong Kong,
or a wild storm
sweeping over the oceans to
New Zealand bush.

Metal arms leap up to imprint
letters on the empty white page.
The ribbon unspools.
The printed page spits out
and she feeds in a new sheet.

The shadow of war lies over Europe now.
China has faded from the news.

But all she can do is write about
the faces of the old Chinese women,
their tiny bound feet,
the mothers and the children
running in terror from the planes
circling overhead, the bombs falling,

the fires, the burnt-out villages,
the lines of trudging refugees,
the little boys and girls,
their curious faces
peeking around the door
as Paul-the-translator gives their names:

Little Horse
Field
Plough
Spade
Miss-Flower-That-We-Eat
Small Moon.

As evening falls and the shadows settle
and bats come out to swoop overhead,
I lie by her side
and I remember
all the places we have lain together:

narrow bunks in ships' cabins
hotel rooms
crowded railway carriages
concrete dugouts
burnt-out buildings
and the open air.

We had adventures,
good times and
very bad times.
We worked hard.
Iris created things –

stories, poems, books, articles,
out of her vast store of words.

What else can I tell you about her?
She hated the dark at night,
always slept with the light on;
loved the whoosh and pull of the sea.
She loved flowers, you know that.

She was brave
unconventional
passionate about the power of words,
used them
shaped them
into new creations.

She wanted – what do we all want? –
to be loved, to be worth loving.
But she could be touchy as a porcupine
and her sharp tongue often scared people away.

Her stiff and crippled body was a burden to her,
the way she had to drag it along on crutches or
leaning on me.
I didn't mind.
I never minded.
I hope she knew that.

She fought injustice
wherever she saw it,
but so much injustice was aimed at her.
If only she had been better paid
for her newspaper work, or paid
at least as much as the men.

If only she had earned more
for her books and poems.
If only she had been paid
the unemployment benefit
when she had no job.

If only *unmarried mother*
had not been such a slur.
If only her health had been better.
Birth control easier.
If only there had been a way.
If only.

Iris, my friend,
I helped you navigate pavements and steps
but I wish I could have helped with the pain as well.
I wish that your life could have been easier
in so many ways.

What will become of me?

All my life,
I have longed for home.
At first I didn't know
where home was.
When I found out,
I missed it even more.

Once, I thought I might see it again.
Now, I know I never will,
but it no longer matters
because now I know
my home is with Iris.

Iris, you took me to places
strange and foreign and enchanting
where I never imagined I would go.

Who knows?
If I had stayed on my island
I might have fallen in a wild storm,
rotted slowly into the ground,
succumbed to disease and crumbled.

I might have been made into a house
or shed, rooted in place
for the rest of my time on earth.
But here I am, a traveller across oceans
and continents,
and blessed with the rare gift of usefulness.

That's how it is.
Some stay. Some leave.

We only flew through the blue sky once
but we sailed over many blue oceans
on all those ships.

Iris, you were so brave.
You were so adventurous.

Iris, my friend,
may your words
live on
forever.

Chinese placenames

The Chinese language is written in characters, which are beautiful and detailed but don't show how to pronounce the words. The pinyin system is a phonetic way to present the words in alphabet form, so they are easier to read and pronounce for people who don't know the characters.

Iris Wilkinson would have known a previous method, which was developed by two Englishmen, Thomas Wade and Herbert Giles. That's why the names she gives for places (and people) are different from placenames on maps today. I've used the names that she would have been familiar with, but here are their modern-day pinyin equivalents:

What Iris called it	*Today it is called*
Peking	Beijing
Shanghai	Shanghai
Canton	Guangzhou
Hankow	Hankou*
Chengchow	Zhengzhou
Hsuchow (or Hsuchowfu)	Xuzhou
Taierhchwang	Taierzhuang
Tsingtao	Qingdao

*merged with Wuchang and Hanyang to form Wuhan

Notes

I took many of the details of Iris Wilkinson's life and her journey through China from her letters home; her China journal; articles by or about her in newspapers and magazines; her *Collected Poems*; pieces published in *Journalese*; in collections of her writing, *Disputed Ground* and *Your Unselfish Kindness*; and her semi-autobiographical novel, *The Godwits Fly*. There is also a comprehensive biography: *The Book of Iris: a life of Robin Hyde* by her son, Derek Challis (AUP, 2002). You don't have to read all of these notes, but you might find some of them interesting. They are also acknowledgements for where I have quoted directly from Robin Hyde's writing.

p. 8: 'Words should be hard old lamps, and white of wick, / And the right flame rises then.' These lines are from a poem called 'Words' that appears in the collection *Houses by the Sea*, published after her death in 1952. Other lines from this poem were chosen to go on the plaque for Robin Hyde / Iris Wilkinson on the Wellington Writers Walk:

> Yet I think, having used my words as the kings used gold,
> Ere we came by the rustling jest of the paper kings,
> I who am overbold will be steadily bold,
> In the counted tale of things.

pp. 10–11: World War Two lasted from 1939–1945, but for the Chinese, war began in 1931 when Japan invaded Manchuria in the north. In 1937 the Marco Polo Bridge incident, near Beijing, sparked the Second Sino-Japanese war ('Sino' means Chinese). Soon Beijing and Tianjin had fallen, then Shanghai and Nanjing, then Wuhan and Canton. The capital was moved from Nanjing to Chongqing, later badly bombed. Japanese troops spread through the country, and millions of Chinese, soldiers and civilians, were killed or made homeless.

The headlines are taken from Australian and New Zealand newspapers on the websites *Trove* and *Papers Past.*

p. 13: Iris describes her birth certificate in her 'Margot' column in the *Wanganui Chronicle*, 1 July 1929.

p. 14: 'Iris can't swim for toffee'. I love this expression! It's from Chapter 4 of her 1934 'Autobiography', which she wrote while at the Grey Lodge, encouraged by Dr Tothill, and is reproduced in *Your Unselfish Kindness*: 'We could neither of us swim for toffee, and she hardly at all … I encouraged her to leave the shallows, because only in deep waters is swimming the heavenly cool sensation that it is. Suddenly she went under, gulped, came up with eyes tightly shut, and flung her sticks of arms (she was very thin) around my neck.'

p. 16: There are lots of advertisements and accounts of end-of-year recitals and concerts for the Culford Bells' classes on *Papers Past.*

'The little Wilkinsons of Waripori Street'. This is from the 1935 'Journal', also written at the Grey Lodge (and can be found in *Your Unselfish Kindness*) dated 28 July: 'An old friend wrote the other day after a lapse of twenty years, calling us "The Little Wilkinsons of Waripori Street." You've no idea what delightful queer old memories that conjured up – little crystal ships, and having hot baths in the copper (we had no bath) and darkest red velvety "pin cushions" growing along the garden borders. It was called "Robin Hood Cottage".'

The house at 92 Northland Road has a Wellington City Council Heritage Plaque on the pavement outside to remember Iris. The plaque calls her: *He wāhine toikupu, kaituhi, kairīpoata* (poet, novelist and journalist). The dedication to her historical novel *Check to your King* reads: 'To the people of a house, 92 Northland Road, Wellington (not forgetting Mulligatawny Dan).' Dan was their dog.

'The wind streaming over the hills'. In her China journal, Iris started a poem about Wellington, especially Northland and Island Bay, and she wrote about 'the wind streaming over Wellington hills'.

p. 17: 'I couldn't help it. I was writing a poem.' This story is from a famous episode in *The Godwits Fly*: 'Half-way through the war, Eliza became a poet.'

p. 18: 'She won second prize in an essay competition open to all the schools of the empire'. The results were announced in the *Evening Post*, 10 January 1922. Her high school must have been very proud of her!

'Schoolgirl poetess at Wellington Girls' College' appeared in the *Dominion*, 31 December 1921.

p. 19: 'Flanders Poppies' appeared in *NZ Freelance*, 26 April 1922. It is signed by 'Iris G.W.'

'Already she felt her poetry as a special, magic gift, / the only thing that was truly hers.' Iris's poem 'The Wonderstone' in the *Wellington Girls' College Reporter* (Vol. 44, No. 72, 1919) contains these lines:

> For God had scattered his gifts divine
> And out of the many, one gift was mine
> […] And my heart leapt up, like a soul set free,
> For the magic gift that had come to me.

In *The Godwits Fly*, Eliza feels that her poetry brings her peace: '… it was the first thing she had ever had that she could truly call her own'.

'The money had to be spent on books'. This is from Chapter 6 of her 1934 'Autobiography', also reproduced in *Your Unselfish Kindness*: 'You had to spend the money on books, but it was Heaven going in to Whitcombe's and buying smooth new desirables – Spenser, Omar,

Keats.' (Whitcombe's was Whitcombe & Tombs, now Whitcoulls.)

p. 23: 'English heather on English hills'. In the first instalment of 'I Travel Alone' in the *Mirror* (May 1938), she writes: 'I want to see an English spring. And the heather.' The article describes her proposed route on the Trans-Siberian and includes the phrase '… chance is the lovely lord of any journey'.

p. 25: The articles Iris wrote for the *New Zealand Railways Magazine* appear from Vol. 10, Issue 1 (1 April 1935) through to Vol. 12, Issue 6 (1 September 1937). They are online at the *New Zealand Electronic Text Collection – Te Pūhikotuhi o Aotearoa.*

p. 26: 'Service car to Paradise'. A service car was a sort of outsized taxi, with extra rows of seats.

p. 29: The Sydney Harbour Bridge took eight years to build and was officially opened in 1932.

p. 31: 'Woman Writer Who Will Cross Siberia'. These details are taken from an article in the Australian newspaper the *Sun*, 23 Jan 1938, p. 10 (which has a photo as well).

'Another Iris, 14 years old, was going home to Hong Kong'. In *Dragon Rampart*, Iris calls her Rene Hsu ('quite alone, and dressed Western style, and all the time she alternated between being twelve years of age and approximately a Chinese five thousand'), but the newspaper article above names her as Iris Koe.

p. 32: The China notebook was given to her by Ronald Holloway, a printer, in October 1935. She wrote in it between Sydney and Hankow, but the first entry is a poem called 'Incidence' about the gift. You can read it online in *Best New Zealand Poems* 2003.

p. 33: 'Good Looks, Good Mechanism, and Good Typing'. There are advertisements for the Hermes Baby portable typewriter on *Papers Past* (e.g. in the *Otago Daily Times*, 10 July 1936, p. 1). I also found a wonderful article titled 'The Extraordinarily Brave and Brilliant Robin Hyde – and her Hermes Baby Portable Typewriter' by Robert Messenger (3 April 2015). bit.ly/3uR7dXT

'She won first prize in the *Sun* Christmas competition for her short story, and second prize for her poem.' You can see the prizewinners listed in the *Sun*, 15 December 1927, on *Papers Past*.

p. 34: There were 12 pennies in a shilling, and 20 shillings in a pound. A guinea was one pound one shilling.

'A genuine poet'. 'The Bookshelf', *Auckland Star*, 30 November 1929, p. 2 (supplement).

'Will be heard of very far away'. 'New books and publications', *Press*, 23 November 1929, p. 13.

'Autumn will run like a boy among the birch trees'. From 'Hanmer Woods'.

'… glory, in a shining sea / Of moonrise, lay on Lambton Quay.' From 'Mists in the City'. You can read these and other poems under 'Robin Hyde' on the *New Zealand Electronic Poetry Centre* website.

p. 35: 'Like me but very much pleasanter'. This is from the 1935 'Journal', also written at the Grey Lodge (and can be found in *Your Unselfish Kindness*), dated 2 March.

'She was elected to PEN, the writers' group'. This meeting was held in the Parliamentary Library and reported in the *Evening Post*, 3 September 1934, p. 3. The new members included prominent New Zealand writers (all men), like RAK Mason, ARD Fairburn, D'Arcy Cresswell and William Satchell. But there are some women mentioned too: Nellie Scanlan, Jane Mander and Jessie Mackay were also well-known writers.

'Unusually versatile, and perhaps the most individual writer this country has produced.'
Evening Post, 18 December 1937, p. 26.

'Am I a cuttlefish, good only for squirting ink?' This is from the 1935 'Journal', also written at the Grey Lodge (and included in *Your Unselfish Kindness*), dated 10 March. 'Must try to save: must dream of more travel – am I a cuttlefish, good only for squirting ink?' Cuttlefish belong to the same class of animals as the squid and octopus, and the ink they produce as a defence mechanism was once widely used for writing and drawing.

p. 39: 'Second class didn't get invited to Captain's Party night but a stewardess snaffled us some treats.' This and other details of the *Changte*'s voyage are told in a series of articles Iris wrote under the banner 'I Travel Alone' for a New Zealand monthly magazine called the *Mirror*.

p. 42: 'Once a Japanese ship slid past, very close. The angry crew wanted to hurl things at it …' Iris wrote a poem called 'Shiplights' about this encounter:

> Hugging the Queensland coast
> There passed us, Saturday night,
> Bare half a mile to port
> A ship tricked out in light;
> […] in clipped stiff English I asked
> What ship, what manner of man?
> And the Chinese boy, watching on,
> Said, a ship of Japan.

p. 50: The whale stranding happened on the night of 16/17 July 1912, when Iris was six. It was described as 'a hundred foot monster' that came ashore after a fierce gale. In the following weekend, thousands of people walked, cycled, drove or caught the tram to go and see it, before it was finally taken off to the meat works. In

The Godwits Fly, Robin Hyde describes the Hannay children 'dancing on a whale washed up at Lyall Bay. Hundreds of children were taken to see it'.

p. 51: Rewi Alley (1897–1987) lived in China for over 60 years, setting up schools, helping Chinese in the countryside to create better working conditions, speaking at peace conferences and travelling in and writing about the country. He encouraged friendship between New Zealand and China, where he was highly regarded and given honorary citizenship.

p. 58: '23746 Sapper George Edward Wilkinson, NZ Army Postal Service (NZ Engineers) 1st NZ Expeditionary Force'. You can find the entry for George Wilkinson on the Auckland War Memorial Museum *Online Cenotaph* website.

'The girls saved their pennies for the Red Cross copper trails, held flower stalls for the Belgian Distress Fund, took part in patriotic concerts.' For example: 'Miss Hazel Wilkinson and friends, by the sale of flowers at Berhampore, raised £1 8s 3d for the Belgian Distress Fund.' *Evening Post*, 26 November 1914, p. 9.

'Hush thee to sleep'. This is one of her earliest poems, written when she was about ten; it appears in *The Godwits Fly*.

'Nellie cried when her brother Bertie was killed at Gallipoli.' You can find the entry for Herbert (Bertie) Augustus Kingsbury Butler on the *Virtual War Memorial Australia* website.

p. 59: 'Always wherever you go, try to make a garden.' This is from a scrapbook that Iris made for Derek in July 1937. It is filled with colourful stickers and some pages have handwritten notes about the stickers, or about her and her sisters' childhood.

p. 68: Pitcairn Island lies in the remote southern Pacific Ocean. Ocean-going liners would stop there on their way between the Panama Canal (opened in 1914) and New Zealand or Australia so their passengers could buy fresh fruit and souvenirs: straw hats, baskets, beads, fans, shell necklaces and wood carvings, including walking sticks. The ships couldn't berth but waited offshore while the islanders came out in small boats, at whatever time of day or night the ships were passing by.

p. 70: In *Passport to Hell*, George Moreton describes how 'a slight woman with an interesting face and a lame leg swung into my office on a walking stick … she laughingly waved her stick as she left my office'. And there is proof that she had a stick when she set off for China, in a photo of her with her friend Kay in Sydney. 'Coconut, miro, orange wood' were used for a Pitcairn Island walking stick now in the collection of the Auckland War Memorial Museum.

p. 71: Of course there is nothing to say that Iris kept the same stick for her whole life, but it's true that her friend Warwick Lawrence recognised her stick as from Pitcairn Island and called it Captain Bligh (incorrectly, because it was not Bligh but Fletcher Christian who came to Pitcairn).

'Blind people hold canes painted white'. Blind people had used sticks for a long time, but white walking canes were first introduced in the early 1930s. In 1933, the New Zealand Institute for the Blind sent them out as gifts as 'the accepted indication throughout New Zealand to motorists and others that the user is a blind person'. The *Chronicle*, May 1933. At first, people carried the canes held out in front of them, to be more easily noticed. You can find more if you look up White Cane Safety Day or explore the website of Blind Low Vision NZ.

p. 72: Iris mentions the walking sticks made from the wood of (or carried by) the *Boyd*, and the Arthur's Pass trampers with their alpenstocks, in her *New Zealand Railways Magazine* articles. 'Old men and women in Whangaroa still carry walking-sticks from the Boyd – not many made from her actual timbers, but more from the cargo of hardwood she was carrying when the Maoris [sic] attacked her.' Vol. 12, Issue 5 (2 August 1937). You can find this online at the *New Zealand Electronic Text Collection – Te Pūhikotuhi o Aotearoa.*

p. 76: 'I want to see the war, not as a chess game / of two opposing armies / but as a *real* crisis that affects *real* people.' This is from 'My journey to the Eastern Front', the first article in a series for *NZ Radio Record*, 26 August 1938.

p. 77: 'The most wonderful trip in the world.' This is from a letter addressed to 'Dear Old Dad' and dated 24 April 1938, Hankow, China.

p. 84: New Zealand women won the vote in 1893, but they weren't allowed to stand for Parliament until 1919. Elizabeth McCombs became the first female MP in 1933. Her husband, James McCombs, was MP for Lyttelton; he died in August 1933, and the Labour Party selected Elizabeth as its candidate for the seat, which she won in the by-election in September.

p. 93: Newspapers of the time record two earthquakes – a light one followed by a sharp, short shock – felt across the lower North Island just before 6 PM on 29 October 1930 (the day Derek was born).

p. 94: The governor-general and his wife arrived in Picton on the evening of 31 October (*Evening Post*, 1 November 1930) so it might have been the next day that Lady Bledisloe visited the hospital.

p. 102: 'Off on the great adventure.' This is the telegram that Timothy wires to Eliza in *The Godwits Fly*.

p. 104: 'Good morning / I can't speak your language'. These lines are from 'Red Pond', published in the *China Journal of Science & Arts*, Vol. 30, 1939.

p. 108: 'Dear Old Mother, Dad, Hazel, Edna and Ruth – and Dan'l the pup'. This is from a letter dated 19 May 1938, Dr Grier's Hospital, Hsuchowfu China. The 'fu' suffix (as in 'Hsuchowfu') had been used in the past to signify the level of administration of an area. It was no longer in official use but was still found on maps, and it was how Robin Hyde sometimes referred to the city in her letters and other writing.

p. 117: 'At night, I heard her weeping / for her lost child.' I took this line from a poem Iris wrote that was published in the *Wellington Girls' College Reporter*, her high school magazine:

> Then the crowd passed on
> And all was silent. But, far-off, I heard
> A lonely mother, weeping for her child …

p. 121: 'She answered letters as Mary Advocate.' These letters and Iris's replies are taken from the Children's Corner in issues of the *NZ Farmers' Advocate* during 1923.

p. 123: Her first published work under her new pen name was a poem called 'Conflagration' on 22 April 1927 in the Christchurch *Sun*.

p. 127: 'In Queenstown, Iris had decided to climb Ben Lomond'. Iris describes this expedition in her *New Zealand Railways Magazine* article: '"I Hear Lake Water Lapping" – The Road to Paradise'. Vol. 12, Issue 1 (1 April 1937). bit.ly/3X6dfk5

p. 139: 'A reporter came to interview Iris'. You can find this interview in the *Newcastle Sun*, Monday 1 August 1938 (page 3). trove.nla.gov.au

p. 141: 'News spread of a huge earthquake in Hawke's Bay'. This was the 1931 Hawke's Bay earthquake, which struck at 10.47 AM on 3 Feb 1931 and measured 7.8 on the Richter scale. More than 250 people died when buildings collapsed and fires swept through them.

p. 145: 'Suicide was not illegal'. Jock Phillips writes in 'Suicide – Preventing suicide' on *Te Ara – the Encyclopedia of New Zealand* that suicide was treated as a crime in British law for centuries. In New Zealand, it stopped being a crime in 1893. However, attempted suicide was still a crime until 1961. About 50 people each year came before the Magistrates Court under this charge, but most were treated leniently and not convicted.

p. 146: 'Auckland Mental Hospital, Avondale'. This was first opened in 1865 as the Whau Lunatic Asylum, afterwards the Avondale Lunatic Asylum. Later, after Iris was there, it became Carrington/Oakley Hospital. Today, the grounds are part of Unitec Institute of Technology.

p. 152: 'No real days, only brief candles of pale light' paraphrases part of a letter from Iris, in England, to another writer, Pat Lawlor, and quoted in the *Dominion*, 10 August 1963. (It was 24 years since Iris's death and Pat Lawlor was trying to interest Wellington people in some kind of memorial to her.)

p. 156: 'Iris would venture anywhere / in search of copy' is a paraphrase of one of Pat Lawlor's articles about

Iris in the *Dominion*, 3 August 1963. He remembered coming across her one night when she was working at the *Wanganui Chronicle*, 'a limping little spectre in search of copy'.

Books by Robin Hyde

Robin Hyde wrote ten books in ten years as well as many poems, short stories and articles.

Non-fiction
Journalese (1934)
A Home in This World (1984)

Travel
Dragon Rampant (1939)

Novels
Check to your King (1936)
Passport to Hell (1936)
Wednesday's Children (1937)
The Godwits Fly (1938)
Nor the Years Condemn (1938)

Poems
The Desolate Star and Other Poems (1929)
The Conquerors and Other Poems (1935)
Persephone in Winter: Poems (1937)
Houses by the Sea (1952)

With *The Conquerors and Other Poems*, Robin Hyde was the first New Zealand writer in the Macmillan's Contemporary Poets series. As well as *Dragon Rampant*, her writing about China includes a number of poems and articles in the *Mirror*, *Woman Today*, *NZ Radio Record* and *Far Eastern Mirror*, among others.

Acknowledgements

Thanks to the NZ Society of Authors, The Cuba Press and (especially) the Solomon family for supporting the NZSA Laura Solomon Cuba Press Prize, established in memory of Laura Solomon, a beloved daughter, sister and aunt and an imaginative and dedicated writer. Mary, Paul and Sarah at The Cuba Press have been a delight to work with and I am grateful for the care and attention they have given this book. Thanks as always to the many wonderful librarians and archivists who have fielded all my queries. Lastly, I would like to acknowledge and pay my respects to Iris Wilkinson /Robin Hyde herself and to the members of her whānau. It has been a privilege to write about her life.

About the author

Philippa Werry is a writer of fiction, non-fiction, poetry and plays. Her interest in history has produced titles such as *Anzac Day*, *Best Mates*, *Waitangi Day*, *Armistice Day*, *Lighthouse Family*, *The New Zealand Wars*, *The Telegram*, *The Water Bottle*, *Quarantine*, *The Other Sister* and *This Is Where I Stand*. *Iris and Me* was the runner-up of the NZSA Laura Solomon Cuba Press Prize 2022. Her work has also appeared in the *School Journal*, educational publications and in various anthologies and has been broadcast on radio. Several of her books have been shortlisted for awards and she is a frequent speaker with the Writers in Schools programme. She lives in Wellington.

Hop on board more Ahoy! stories

Winner of the NZSA Laura Solomon Cuba Press Prize 2022.

'Rachel Fenton has woven comics deeply into her story to magical and powerful effect.'
– Mat Tait, author of *Te Wehenga*

Sequel to Book Award finalist *Slice of Heaven*.

'A great portrait of the community of South Auckland and of a school culture ... If you miss this one you will kick yourself.' – Bob Docherty

By the author of award-winning *The Discombobulated Life of Summer Rain*.

'Heartwarming coming-of-age story'
– KidsBooksNZ

Winner of NZSA Best First Book, NZ Book Awards for Children 2022.

'The writing is exceptional, the story's a ripper ... we're reminded of Jack Lasenby' – *The Spinoff*